JEALOUSY AND JUSTICE

Jealousy and Justice

The indigenous roots of colonial rule
in northern Sulawesi

David Henley

VU Uitgeverij, Amsterdam 2002

Editorial Note

This 22nd volume of the Comparative Asian Studies Series of the Amsterdam School for Social Science Research (ASSR) and VU University Press concludes the publication of the series. The series has offered to a wide public, in South and Southeast Asia as well as in Europe and elsewhere, a rich collection of publications that deal with processes in Asia from a comparative and socio-historical vantage point. The editorial committee felt obliged to reconsider the future of the CAS-series in its present form because of the convergence of several developments: changes in the publication policy of VU University Press, an expansion in the scope of activities of the Asian Studies programme in Amsterdam, and the departure of the present editor for a professorial post at Wageningen University. There is a good possibility that the Asian Studies programme in Amsterdam will publish results in a different format in the future. You may contact the AsiA website (www.pscw.uva.nl/asia) for further information.

Leontine Visser,
General Editor

VU University Press is an imprint of
VU Boekhandel/Uitgeverij bv
De Boelelaan 1105
1081 HV Amsterdam
The Netherlands

Layout by Sjoukje Rienks, Amsterdam

The illustrations in this publication are reproduced by permission of Leiden University Library and the Algemeen Rijksarchief (General Archive), The Hague.

isbn 90-5383-795-7
nur 653

© VU University Press / CASA–ASiA, Amsterdam, 2002

All rights reserved. No part of this publication may be reproduced, stored in a retrieval system, or transmitted, in any form or by any means, mechanically, by photocopying, recording, or otherwise, without written permission of the holder of the copyright.

Contents

1	Introduction	9
2	Northern Sulawesi and the Dutch	13
3	Social origins of colonial power	23
4	The problem of jealousy	33
5	The problem of justice	37
6	Warfare, ritual, and collective action	43
7	The rebel's dilemma	49
8	The stranger-king and his alternatives	53
9	Indigenous states, indigenous strangers	61
10	Civility, faith, and the wages of sin	69
11	Patterns and parallels	75
12	Concluding remarks	83
	Abbreviations	91
	Bibliography	93

'And in all places, where men have lived by small Families, to robbe and spoyle one another, has been a Trade, and [...] the greater spoyles they gained, the greater was their honour; and men observed no other Lawes therein, but the Lawes of Honour; that is, to abstain from cruelty, leaving to men their lives, and instruments of husbandry.'

'The finall Cause, End, or Designe of men, (who naturally love Liberty, and Dominion over others,) in the introduction of that restraint upon themselves, (in which wee see them live in Commonwealths,) is the foresight of their own preservation, and of a more contented life thereby; that is to say, of getting themselves out from that miserable condition of Warre, which is necessarily consequent [...] to the naturall Passions of men, when there is no visible Power to keep them in awe [...]'

'[N]o man in any Cause ought to be received for Arbitrator, to whom greater profit, or honour, or pleasure apparently ariseth out of the victory of one party, than of the other: for hee hath taken (though an unavoydable bribe, yet) a bribe; and no man can be obliged to trust him. And thus also the controversie, and the condition of War remaineth [...]'

Thomas Hobbes, *Leviathan* (1996 [1651]: 109, 117, 118)

1 Introduction

Historians of Indonesia often think of states, and especially colonial states, as predatory institutions encroaching aggressively on the territory and autonomy of freedom-loving stateless peoples. Gullick (1958: 28-9) and Adas (1981: 232-3), for instance, argued that for a long time the only really effective check on the rapacity of Malay and Javanese rulers was the circumstance that disaffected subjects ultimately had the option of fleeing to uninhabited areas beyond state control. For Barbara and Leonard Andaya, early European expansion in Sumatra and the Moluccas was synonymous with the distortion or destruction of decentralised indigenous political systems based on cooperation, alliance, economic complementarity, and myths of common ancestry (B.W. Andaya 1993; L.Y. Andaya 1993). Anthony Reid (1997: 81) describes tribal societies like those of the Batak and Minangkabau in highland Sumatra as 'miracles of statelessness' which 'defended their autonomy by a mixture of guerilla warfare, diplomatic flexibility, and deliberate exaggeration of myths about their savagery' until ultimately overwhelmed by Dutch military power. Before colonialism, in this view, most Indonesians relied for security not on the protection of a powerful king, but on a 'complex web of contractual mutualities' embodying a 'robust pluralism' (Reid 1998b: 29, 32). 'So persistently', concludes Reid (1997: 80-81), 'has each step towards stronger states in the archipelago arisen from trading ports, with external aid and inspiration, that one is inclined to seek the indigenous political dynamic in a genius for managing without states'. Henk Schulte Nordholt, for his part, cautions against any tendency to downplay the violent, repressive aspects of colonial and post-colonial government in Indonesia, and urges historians of the country 'to wrest themselves free from the interests, perspective, and cognitive framework of the state' (Schulte Nordholt 2000: 29). An even more systematic attempt to demonise the (modern) state in Indonesia and elsewhere can be found in the work of James Scott (1998a, 1998b).

Views like these, of course, have a whole variety of distinguished intellectual pedigrees, from Rousseau through Marx to Foucault. Among contemporary Indonesians, however, their popularity is strikingly limited. That this should be the case in places where no memory survives of a time when people 'managed without' the state is perhaps not surprising. Appreciation for the advantages of life under state control, however, is also to be found among groups which still stood outside such control less than a century ago. Lauje hill farmers in the remote hinterland of Tinombo in Central Sulawesi, for example, recently surprised anthropologist Tania Li (2001: 50) by describing the time of their ancestors as 'one dominated by fear' and crediting the colonial and Indonesian states with resolving tensions and feuds which had formerly made travel dangerous and subsistence insecure.

> 'Dutch rule [...] offered a partial solution to these problems. Hill folk recalled: "In the old days there was fighting because people were not afraid of the government. Now it is safe because the government is strong [...]." [...] Conditions of violence are still said to prevail in the more distant headwaters, where government is weak, and people express a fear that violence will re-emerge [...]. [A] conception of themselves as headstrong people [...] who need outside authority if they are to form communities and live at peace with one another, is deeply embedded in hillside identities [...]'. (Li 2001: 51)

In this essay I examine the process of state formation, and in particular the expansion of the colonial state, in the northern half of Sulawesi, where the precolonial background was one of endemic competition and violent conflict. Stateless communities in this region were not only highly vulnerable to incorporation into colonial power systems, but often requested such incorporation themselves. In the first place this was because their chronic insecurity in the face of both foreign and local enemies inclined them to accept offers of military assistance from virtually any quarter. In addition, however, I will argue that in many cases there was also a degree of collective, consensual readiness on the part of a number of rival groups to accept a common political and judicial authority.[1] Indigenous leaders, far from possessing a 'genius for managing without states', possessed a near-Hobbesian awareness of the inevitability of conflict in tribal life and the desirability of a certain amount of state intervention to alleviate this problem. At

---

1 Existing attempts to identify the indigenous foundations of colonial expansion, by contrast, have usually emphasised 'collaboration' by (typically small and selfish) elite groups among the colonised (Adas 1993: 319-23; Robinson 1972; Scammell 1980).

the same time, their mutual jealousy and distrust made it easier for them to accept outsiders (whose lack of local blood ties was supposed to help guarantee their impartiality) in the roles of arbitrators, judges, and enforcers of the peace than it was to create indigenous institutions with the same functions. In tandem with the role of foreigners as traders, and hence as distributors of valuable and prestigious foreign goods, this logic of jealousy and justice probably goes a long way toward explaining the importance of 'stranger-kings' (Indonesian as well as European) in the history of Indonesia.[2]

Like most other stateless peoples, those of northern Sulawesi left very little written documentation from which to reconstruct their actions and intentions. Three circumstances, however, help to compensate for this historiographic handicap. The European (mostly Dutch) historical sources for the region, firstly, are numerous and detailed, covering a timespan of more than three centuries and in many cases including direct quotations from indigenous informants. If the moralistic tendency in late-colonial and missionary accounts sometimes threatens to interfere with their substance, secondly, this is less true of the earlier writings of Dutch East India Company (VOC) officials, most of whom had no concern to justify their actions in terms of any supposed needs or aspirations of the indigenous people with whom they came into contact. The very detailed but sometimes partisan ethnographies of Central Sulawesi by missionary-anthropologists Albert Kruyt (1869-1949), Nicolaus Adriani (1865-1926), and Albert's son Jan Kruyt (1893-1978), for instance, are counterbalanced by the witty and dispassionate realism of Robert Padtbrugge (1637-1703), a Leiden-trained physician turned VOC governor of Ternate who left lucid and anthropologically insightful accounts of his three visits to North Sulawesi in the years 1677-82.[3] Most of the patterns and processes reconstructed below, thirdly, are too clearly and consistently evident in the historical record to result simply from bias in the sources. My aim here, I should add, is indeed to identify certain recurrent historical patterns, and not to attempt a complete interpretation, still less a complete description, of state formation in northern Sulawesi. By exhuming some particular home truths of colonial history, nevertheless, we can perhaps help illuminate those tensions between freedom and equality on the one hand, and order and justice on the other, which are no less relevant to Indonesia today than they were to the war-torn England of Hobbes' time.

---

2 The phenomenon of the stranger-king is classically discussed in a Pacific context by Marshall Sahlins (1985: 73-103). Leonard Andaya (1993: 65-6, 174, 240) and James Fox (1995: 217-9) point out the strong parallels in eastern Indonesian political systems; Fernandéz-Armesto (2000: 87-90) and Oosten (1988) provide broader comparative perspectives.
3 Data on the lives and intellectual backgrounds of these men are provided by Koentjaraningrat (1975: 49-51), Pabbruwe (1994), and Schrauwers (2000: 51-8).

2 Northern Sulawesi and the Dutch

In the seventeenth and early eighteenth centuries the Dutch East India Company expanded from its base on the clove-producing island of Ternate to become the dominant power in the northern half of Sulawesi, a region which yielded almost no precious spices and was of economic value only for the small quantities of rice, gold, iron, turtleshell and forest products which it exported to the Moluccas. By 1750 this peripheral area contained a dozen VOC forts, strung out over a distance of some 800 km from Parigi, near Palu in Central Sulawesi, to Tabukan in the Sangir islands between Manado and the Philippines. Another century later, the Dutch colonial state exercised direct rule over a total of perhaps 175,000 people in Minahasa and Gorontalo, obliging 100,000 Minahasans to spend up to half of their working time on compulsory coffee cultivation and roadbuilding duties; in Sangir, Talaud, Bolaang-Mongondow, and parts of Central Sulawesi, the leaders of at least another 200,000 people acknowledged its formal sovereignty. In 1910, by which time the whole of Central Sulawesi had also been brought under its authority, the colonial administrative residency of Manado controlled and taxed a population of almost a million souls inhabiting a territory the size of Portugal.

Except for the aggressive military actions which completed the colonisation of Central Sulawesi at the beginning of the twentieth century, no episode in this remarkable process of expansion was initiated unilaterally by the Dutch themselves. Throughout the seventeenth, eighteenth, and nineteenth centuries, the VOC and colonial authorities in Manado and Ternate regularly received unsolicited invitations from all over northern Sulawesi to establish new outposts.[4] While many of these requests for garrisons were prudently refused, the Dutch did tend to extend their formal suzerainty over any polity, however small, which desired an individual alliance. By the second half of the eighteenth century, consequently, fully one quarter of all the political treaties signed by the VOC anywhere in Asia were being concluded with the economically insignificant chiefdoms of northern Sulawesi (CD VI: V-XI).

Indeed, the Company sometimes had more difficulty extracting itself from existing involvements than initiating new ones. In 1615, for example, its representatives in the Moluccas, learning that the sergeant in charge of their new outpost on Siau (Sangir) had complied with a request from Manado for soldiers to help protect the Manadonese against exactions by the sultanate of Ternate, promptly reversed this unauthorised decision in order to avoid antagonising the Ternatans. The expedition despatched to Manado with orders 'to withdraw our people from that place by one means or another', according to its commander, was able to accomplish this only 'with great risk to their lives, leaving behind 180 lb of gunpowder as well as some other inconsequential property which the inhabitants would not allow them to take with them' (Tiele and Heeres 1886-95, I: 133). In 1795, comparably, a naval force sent to withdraw the remote and entirely unprofitable VOC garrison in Parigi succeeded by a fluke of luck in recovering the guns and other equipment from the fort despite the determination of the local population 'to resist this by all possible means' (Colenbrander 1898: 591), but was unable to bring home its commanding officer and two other soldiers, who were detained by angry chiefs and never seen again.

Northern Sulawesi was inhabited mostly by stateless societies in which kinship and gift-exchange were the main principles of political organisation, and confederacies of intermarrying villages the largest units capable of sustained political solidarity.[5] 'The Dutch', as anthropologist Mieke Schouten (1998: 72) has noted, 'did not even have to bother to implement a policy of divide and rule: the division existed before their arrival'. Minahasa, for instance, contained more than 20 such village federations speaking eight different languages, and during the period of heavy corvée labour impositions in the nineteenth century, several European observers commented that it was largely 'the dissention and jealousy existing between the various districts' (De Clercq 1870a: 127) which made anti-

---

4 In some cases, the local leaders in question explicitly added that their communities were fully prepared to pay the costs of their own occupation (ARA VOC 1775: 108; Bleeker 1856: 129).
5 A single village typically consisted of several exogamous 'big houses', each containing a group of matrilaterally-related nuclear families which shared a common inheritance of valuable goods - textiles, brassware, porcelain, livestock, and sometimes also farmland (Chabot 1969: 95; Schrauwers 2000: 67; Van Wouden 1941: 410).

colonial resistance impossible.⁶ In some places larger chiefdoms, often based on control of harbour settlements and headed by 'kings' (Malay: *raja*; in local languages: *datu, kolano, mokole*) were also present, but their influence was limited and their mutual relations, like those of their vassals, frequently violent. In 1569, a Portuguese Jesuit already identified North Sulawesi as a 'restless' area and attributed this to its division between 'so many kings' (H. Jacobs 1974-84, I: 525). Seventeenth-century writers agreed that the Sangirese were 'habitually at odds with one another' (J. Hustaart, Schriftelijk vertoog tegenwoordigen staat Moluxe eijlanden 1656, in KITLV H454e) and the Minahasans a particularly fractious and warlike people:

> 'Because of the many kings and headmen which they have in this country, there are diverse factions, conflicts and feuds. [...] Their arms are spears, cuirasses, and swords [...]. They fight their wars on land, against each other; in war they are cruel, putting to death all who submit to them, without granting them life or captivity. Their greatest triumph is to hang up in their doorways the skulls of those they have killed.' (Colin 1900 [1660]: 111.)

Intercommunal warfare, as this Spanish account suggests, was institutionalised by headhunting traditions embedded in ritual and religion (Downs 1955: 40-51; Schouten 1992) and perpetuated by hereditary feuds.⁷

The condition of statelessness, needless to say, fell well short of the deadly anarchy or 'war of every man against every man' which Hobbes, more for the sake of logical clarity than with any ethnographic pretentions, counterposed at some points in *Leviathan* to the peace and order of his absolutist 'Commonwealth'.⁸ Headhunting wars, fought between shifting coalitions of scattered village communities, were typically small-scale, intermittent affairs, and their overall effects on mortality seem to have been slight compared with those of disease and poor nutrition (Henley, in press). Albert Kruyt (1895: 109), although keen to see them suppressed, likened them to 'guerilla' conflicts rather than to the bloody national confrontations of Europe, and later (1938, II: 56) even characterised them in retrospect as 'a sort of sport' in which young men had participated during the agricultural off-season. One reason for the limited character of

---

6 Also: Schouten 1998: 72; J.J. ten Siethoff, Topografische schetsen Manado 1845 (ANRI Manado 46).
7 Adriani and Kruyt 1912-14, I: 202-6; A.C. Kruyt 1930: 506-7; 1938, I: 168.
8 Hobbes, as Marshall Sahlins (1968: 7) points out, did not believe that 'primitive anarchy' had ever been a 'general empirical condition'; reading *Leviathan*, in fact, it is clear that like Sahlins, Hobbes (1996: 88-9) saw 'Warre' less as the enduring condition of stateless political systems than as their underlying 'inclination' or 'disposition'.

these wars was that in some degree they were usually subject to 'Lawes of Honour' of the type which Hobbes, contrary to common belief, attributed even to stateless peoples. Robert Padtbrugge, a contemporary of Hobbes, gave a firsthand account of how such customary restrictions affected tribal warfare in Minahasa:

> 'The defeated party becomes completely subject to the victors and must dance to their tune, retaining only the rice which it has stored in its houses, while any standing crops are destroyed. The winners, however, take great care not to destroy the stored rice and will therefore also refrain from burning down defeated villages, which if it does happen is usually the work of Europeans participating in the attack. Women and children, finally, are carried away as prisoners, but readily released, with or without a ransom payment, after peace has been restored. Any men who do not manage to escape, on the other hand, are all killed, regardless of age.' (Padtbrugge 1866 [1679]: 318.)

Other and perhaps more important mitigating factors, as a later Dutch administrator observed in Central Sulawesi, arose simply from the limited organisational and economic capabilities of the societies in question, which lacked either the centralised authority necessary to raise large armies, or the accumulated resources with which to sustain long military campaigns.

> 'They are constantly at war with their neighbours, robbing and plundering each other, so that security is an unknown concept. Yet in recent years there have been few cases of complete conquest and subjugation of one kingdom by another. For this their military strength is insufficient, and their subjects too unwilling to engage in lengthy wars, restricting themselves instead to occasional raids and expeditions lasting a few days.' (AV Oostkust Celebes 1850, in ANRI Ternate 180.)

The overall impact of violence on the life of these stateless peoples, nevertheless, must not be underestimated. However limited the scale of their wars, they still 'lived more in war than in peace' (Adriani and Kruyt 1912-14, I: 200), and in upland areas almost the only way to avoid regular violence was to avoid regular contact with any non-kinsmen by living a life of flight, isolation, and dishonour on the infertile frontiers of settlement. Among groups which chose to stand their ground in densely-populated areas of high agricultural value such as the central plateau of Minahasa, a homicide record was an essential criterion of social status for men, and every boy was encouraged from an early age to display the qualities of bravery and cunning which would make him a good killer (Schouten

1995: 13). When witches were executed, or human sacrifices made to avert natural disasters, seal alliances, or glorify the life-cycle ceremonies of influential people, children participated 'in order to get accustomed in a safe way to the sight of flowing blood and to the hacking of human flesh' (Adriani and Kruyt 1950-51, II: 434).[9]

Even those minimal rules of honourable combat described by Padtbrugge, moreover, must be interpreted as normative ideals rather than binding restrictions; many other sources indicate that women and children were often killed by headhunters, and villages readily put to the torch.[10] Most nuclear settlements, accordingly, were built in strategic locations and more or less permanently fortified, while the need for any party venturing outside them to include armed men was a constant hindrance to agriculture and commerce. Women, in striking contrast to the traditional pattern of female commercial activity in more peaceful Southeast Asian societies (Reid 1988-93, I: 163-5), could play little or no role in trade; many, indeed, never left their home villages (Adriani and Kruyt 1912-14, II: 301). Endemic violence also coloured social and political life in more unexpected ways. If the particularly warlike To Napu of Lore in upland Central Sulawesi were known as the 'dogs' of a lowland *raja* in the Palu valley, for example, this was not because they showed any special obedience to him on a routine basis, but because as keen headhunters, they were always ready to act as his 'hunting dogs' by carrying out punitive raids in his name (A.C. Kruyt 1938, I: 256). The value which people attached to a written 'pass' or travel permit issued by the Dutch authorities derived not from any freedom from technical travel restrictions (which were usually impossible to enforce), but rather from 'the conviction that the Government will avenge the death of the bearer should anyone kill him' (Adriani and Kruyt 1912-14, I: 183).[11]

Indigenous violence was exacerbated by the predatory activities of outsiders, notably Bugis and Muslim Filipino slave-raiders, and in the seventeenth century also by the competitive intervention of major powers such as Ternate, Makassar, and the European spice traders themselves; one of the main reasons why the VOC committed itself to involvement in the region was in order to expel its Spanish rivals, the last of whom eventually left in 1677. Initial requests from indigenous leaders for Dutch intervention were typically inspired by a desire for

---

9   Also: Aragon 2000: 235; A.C. Kruyt 1938, III: 480; IV: 132; Sarasin and Sarasin 1905, II: 123-5; Woensdregt 1930: 599.
10 Adriani 1913: 862; Adriani and Kruyt 1912-14, I: 213; II: 398; 1950-51, I: 317; Van der Crab 1875: 365; De Clercq 1870b: 5; Godée Molsbergen 1928: 124; GM III: 327; A.C. Kruyt 1899: 185; 1938, I: 56, 77, 81, 108, 129, 300, 302; Padtbrugge 1866: 319; Sarasin and Sarasin 1905, II: 90.
11 Indigenous chiefs sometimes also issued written passes of this kind (GM IX: 139; Ulfers 1868: 12).

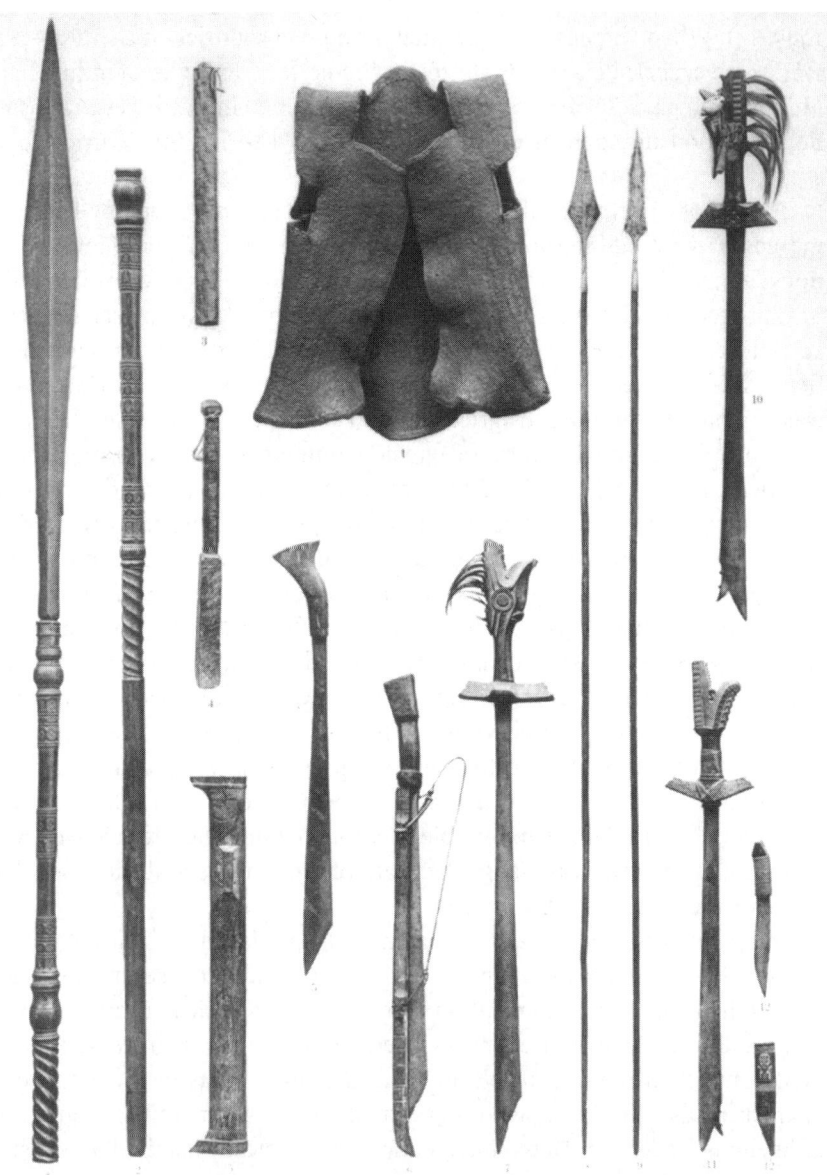

Arms and armour from Minahasa and Talaud. Source: Meyer and Richter 1903, Tafel I.

military assistance, whether against local enemies, foreign aggressors, or both (Henley 1993: 41-6). The decision to establish a permanent VOC presence in Manado in 1656, for instance, followed a plea by the raja of Tabukan (Sangir) for Dutch help in a complex conflict between himself, Ternate, Tagulandang (also in

Shields and armour from Minahasa. The helmet is of VOC origin. Source: Meyer and Richter 1903, Tafel II.

Sangir) and the *raja* of Manado on the one hand, and Siau together with some upland Minahasan groups, backed by the Spanish, on the other (ARA VOC 1211: 894v). The decisive Dutch attack on Gorontalo in 1681 was launched partly on behalf of Tomini and Dumoga, two small neighbouring chiefdoms which had managed to attract VOC support in their struggle against Gorontalese expansion by declaring an intention to convert to Christianity (Van Dam 1931: 87). When Gorontalo itself requested a permanent Dutch garrison in 1729, its intention was primarily to reinforce its control of local gold production in the face of threats from Bugis and Magindanao (Filipino) interlopers (Henley 1997: 425). In 1751, the *raja* of Parigi declared himself a Dutch vassal and his kingdom a 'loan' from the VOC after a Company sea patrol brought to heel a 'rebel' who had been causing him trouble (CD V: 526).

That the attraction of Company military backing for indigenous allies was a key aspect of early Dutch expansion in Indonesia is a familiar argument in the general literature on the VOC (E.M. Jacobs 2000: 213; Vos 1993: 208). Yet whatever made the Dutch attractive as a military ally in northern Sulawesi, it does not seem to have been their numerical strength. In 1669 there were only 32 VOC soldiers in the main Dutch outpost, Manado (ARA VOC 1271: 589), and a century later the whole of Minahasa was reported to be 'governed, guarded, and kept in order' by a total of 47 Company personnel, including the Dutch resident himself, two bookkeepers, a surgeon, an interpreter, a shipwright, four schoolmasters, a church warden, and 36 soldiers (J.L. Seydelman, Memorie Manado en aangrenzende rijken 1769, in ARA VOC 3301). In 1855 there were still only 43 soldiers in Manado, and the defensive works there and elsewhere in Minahasa were said to be in a 'deplorable condition'. 'And with this tiny force', marvelled a visiting official from Batavia, 'we control 80,000 natives, inhabiting a land area of 125 square [German] miles [6,800 km^2]!' (Fragment 1856: 2, 7).[12] In 1821 the naturalist Reinwardt (1858: 507) wrote that with its total strength of 13 men, the military garrison in the other major Dutch 'stronghold' in the region, Gorontalo, was 'hardly sufficient to maintain a regular watch, let alone to be of any use for defensive purposes'.[13]

If strength of numbers is hardly credible as a factor here, neither should the European advantage in terms of military technology be exaggerated. Firearms, including cannon, were already present in the area in small numbers during the sixteenth century, well before the arrival of the VOC (Blair and Robertson 1903: 69). By the late seventeenth they had become quite commonplace; when Padtbrugge visited Gorontalo in 1677, his party was greeted by an honour guard including 'twelve musketeers who were reasonably well practiced with their

---

[12] The first figure is an underestimate, the second a mild exaggeration; the real area of Minahasa is about 5,300 km^2.

[13] Another puzzled visitor was inclined to explain the paradox of military weakness and political strength to 'the great moral influence which the Netherlands [Indies] Government excercises in these regions' (Olivier 1937: 10).

weapons, as was apparent from the three salvos fired upon the arrival of the Governor, which proceeded in a very good and orderly fashion' (Van der Aa 1867: 148).[14] Not until the nineteenth century were the Dutch able, or even concerned, to limit the possession of firearms in the areas under their authority. When preparations for such control were finally made in Gorontalo in 1824, an initial survey counted 476 small arms and 134 heavier weapons in local hands; the real numbers were no doubt larger (AV Gorontalo 1824, in ANRI Gorontalo 3).[15] On land, the European advantage in terms of weaponry was still slighter than is generally assumed even during the final colonial conquests at the beginning of the twentieth century, when many men in Central Sulawesi possessed breech-loading and even repeating rifles (including American Winchesters) imported by Bugis traders.[16] At sea, admittedly, steam gunboats had by this stage made the Dutch lead overwhelming. In earlier periods, however, colonial naval forces were outnumbered, outmanoeuvred, and sometimes even outgunned by those of indigenous 'pirates', particularly slave raiders from the southern Philippines. During the heyday of the Sulu sultanate from 1770 to 1850, as Warren (1981: 164) has shown, 'the Iranun and Balangingi, not the Dutch, were the true lords of the eastern seas'.

---

14 Later in the same visit, one of the Gorontalo *raja* eagerly quizzed Padtbrugge on 'the design, manufacture, and properties of petards, mortars, grenades, trenches, and especially siege-mining' (Van der Aa 1867: 161).
15 The effectiveness of muzzle-loading small arms, with their very low rate of fire, was in any case limited under Southeast Asian conditions; in Central Sulawesi the most practiced warriors reportedly viewed them with 'contempt', preferring their traditional javelins and bladed weapons (Adriani and Kruyt 1912-14, II: 191).
16 Goedhart 1908: 537, 489; Hissink 1912: 114; A.C. Kruyt 1892: 247.

3) Social origins of colonial power

If the Europeans were small in number and their armaments less than formidable, the fact remains that military factors were by no means irrelevant to early European expansion in northern Sulawesi. Small detachments of VOC soldiers quite often joined a local ally in a raid on a mutual enemy, and very occasionally Dutch forces also participated in a bigger military action. In some cases even these major interventions bore more relation to Indonesian than to Dutch interests, and had few lasting consequences. The governor of Ternate who sent two VOC ships to support a bloody but indecisive Ternatan intervention in a Gorontalese civil war in 1647, for instance, was reprimanded by his superiors in Batavia for diverting resources from the struggle with the Spanish over Moluccan spices into an economically pointless and 'very hazardous' exploit guaranteed to antagonise powerful Makassar, which at that time claimed sovereignty over Gorontalo (Tiele and Heeres 1886-95, III: 358-9, 388-90).[17] There were defeats too: although some VOC fortifications were of high quality, and the one at Manado withstood a major attack by a Magindanao (Sulu) war fleet in 1777 (Riedel 1864a: 520-22), several of the smaller wooden forts built by the Company in remote gold-producing areas were overrun by Indonesian (mostly Bugis and Mandar) enemies in the course of the eighteenth century.[18] On four occasions prior to the

---

17 The most spectacular 'naive' intervention of this kind occurred in 1856 when Tobungku, a remote vassal state of Ternate on the east coast of Central Sulawesi, persuaded the Dutch to organise a 900-man Dutch-Ternatan expedition against its local enemy Mori, an inland chiefdom of no significance to the Europeans (Uhlenbeck 1861; Weitzel 1883).
18 These events are described in the memories van overgave of the VOC governors of Ternate edited by Niemeijer (forthcoming).

twentieth century, nevertheless, successful Dutch-inspired and Dutch-led military expeditions did shape the political future of the region in a decisive way.

In 1661, firstly, one part of upland Minahasa, Tondano, defied its new Dutch masters and was attacked by the VOC. So many other Minahasans joined in this attack, however, that with their help just 65 VOC soldiers quickly compelled the rebel force of fully 1,400 men to surrender.[19] In 1677, governor Padtbrugge brought together assorted enemies of the *raja* of Siau—other Sangir and Sulawesi chiefs who had suffered from Siau raiding, a disaffected noble from Siau itself, and a sultan of Ternate insulted by the *raja*'s recent marriage to a former wife of his—for a joint attack on Siau and its small Spanish garrison, the last in Indonesia. The island was duly conquered by 500 Indonesian warriors, nine of whom died, and meekly transferred to VOC sovereignty without the accompanying Dutch vessels having to fire a shot. The governor's main task on this expedition was one of planning and coordination: to ensure, in his own words, that his allies did not 'wander in there like a flock of sheep [...] or start quarrelling with each other' (Van der Aa 1867: 180). Four years later Padtbrugge and 40 Dutch soldiers, together with 1,300 Sangirese, Sulawesi and Moluccan auxiliaries, ended Gorontalo's hopes of regional dominance by capturing and destroying its recently rebuilt estuarine fort. Both sides used firearms and light artillery; this time the Indonesian allies apparently played little part in the final assault, but the defenders made the mistake of attempting to rush the advancing European infantry instead of remaining in the safety of their stronghold; a total of 29 Gorontalese and five attackers died.[20] In 1809, finally, hundreds of Moluccan, Minahasan and European troops ended the last serious anticolonial resistance in Minahasa by defeating a second rebellion in Tondano. This 'Tondano War' was a longer and bloodier conflict of which more will be said below; once again, superior discipline and greater numbers of indigenous allies were the main factors in the government victory.

In so far as military factors were decisive here, in other words, they related in the first place to organisational rather than technological abilities, and represented only one aspect of a more general superiority with respect to social solidarity and coordination. The Company, for instance, could always be relied upon not to disintegrate into warring factions as a result of internal disagreements, and if its actual strength in the region was usually unimpressive, it was potentially capable of drawing reinforcements in greater numbers and from further

---

19 GM III: 384-5; Godée Molsbergen 1928: 18-19, 64. The rebels, moreover, were well fortified in the pile village of Tondano on the lake of the same name.

20 *Dagh-register* 1681: 587; GM IV: 514; Godée Molsbergen 1928: 83-4. The fort, containing 900 men and 11 artillery pieces, had earth-filled stone walls 3 m thick and 2.5 m high, surmounted by a bamboo pallisade (ARA VOC 1366: 893).

afield than any local power. To some extent this superiority was a result of advanced administrative techniques unknown in indigenous society, including bureaucratic rules which were at once systematically enforced and subject to deliberate modification as the circumstances demanded. As far as the ethnic Europeans themselves were concerned, it also drew strength from the fact that as members of a small foreign minority with relatively few local blood ties and a strong sense of its own superiority, white VOC personnel and colonial officials were seldom tempted to defect from their collective undertakings by siding with indigenous parties for reasons of kinship or opportunism.[21] In terms of the ability of the same minority to attract the allegiance of other groups, a third important factor was of course its access to economic resources. State formation in island Southeast Asia, as many historians have emphasised, was often closely associated with the control and distribution of valuable trade goods, by means of which aspiring elites were able to create debt and dependency.[22] Until late in the nineteenth century the Dutch in northern Sulawesi, like the chiefs of its indigenous harbour settlements, extracted the export goods which they desired (principally rice, gold, and coffee) not as a form of pure tribute or taxation, but in politically regulated exchange for imported textiles, iron, and cash.

The idea that economic exchange was a key basis for political expansion in the Dutch case, on the other hand, is called into serious question by the fact that while the Dutch were often a preferred military ally, they were seldom a preferred trading partner. In order to maximise their profits and defray the costs of their military and administrative establishments, both the VOC and the colonial state which superseded it usually required that tributary exchange took place on terms which were highly disadvantageous for their local subjects. In the early nineteenth century, for example, the ratio between the prices paid for gold and coffee by the Dutch government, and those which could be obtained for the same products from private traders, was typically about 2:3, and sometimes lower (Van Doren 1860: 371; L. Wessels 1891: 51, 56). Where possible, consequently, producers resorted to extensive 'smuggling'. In Gorontalo, where gold exports were technically subject to a Dutch monopoly, it was estimated in 1846 that three times the amount of gold delivered to the government was being shipped to Singapore by Bugis traders (Francis 1860: 339), whose lower overheads and greater responsiveness to local tastes in import goods enabled them to offer more attractive

---

21 A parallel here is the way in which the effectiveness of trading minorities in Indonesia, particularly the ethnic Chinese, has benefited from their social isolation. The prospect of expulsion into a culturally alien and often hostile host society, it has been argued, makes defection from commercial agreements and conventions less tempting (Dewey 1962: 46-9).
22 A particularly detailed presentation of this argument has recently been provided by Junker (1999: 3-28, 373-86) with respect to the Philippines.

prices.²³ Yet Dutch political authority in Gorontalo, at least during the nineteenth century, was never seriously threatened as a result of this formidable commercial competition. The resident Bugis community, indeed, provided part of the armed militia which helped defend the outpost, and in 1827 participated in the suppression a minor local revolt.²⁴ Far from fearing that trade wealth would enable the Bugis to usurp their own position, local Dutch officials saw themselves as helping to maintain the peace between mutually hostile Bugis and Gorontalese elites (AV Gorontalo 1854, in ANRI Gorontalo 3).

This mediating role of the Dutch authorities in Gorontalo was not limited to inter-ethnic relations, but also extended to those between the five segmentary chiefdoms or 'kingdoms' (*rijken*) making up the loose confederacy (known as the *Lima lo Pohalaa* or 'Five Alliances') to which the whole of the indigenous Gorontalese population belonged. 'The kingdoms appear to live in good harmony with each other', states one report from 1852, 'but this would quickly change if the official in charge of the division were not careful to ensure that the conflicts which now and then arise over land, tree crops, inheritances, and so forth were immediately investigated and resolved' (AV Gorontalo 1852, in ANRI Gorontalo 3). That such external conflict resolution was indeed important is suggested by a source from a period at the beginning of the nineteenth century when it was temporarily unavailable. In 1805, seven years after Gorontalo was abandoned by the Dutch in connection with British military action in the Moluccas, high-ranking Gorontalese envoys to the remaining outpost in Manado 'complained bitterly about the constant disorder prevailing in their villages, of which they predicted the direst consequences', and begged for the re-establishment of a small garrison 'to bring some improvement in their deplorable situation' (Resident Manado to Governor Ternate, 12.10.1805, in ANRI Manado 60).

At first sight, it is tempting to dismiss these claims as expressions of colonial self-importance and aristocratic power-lust respectively. The functional complementarity implied here between indigenous statelessness and colonial state-formation, however, is part of a widespread and recurrent pattern. Repeatedly in the historical sources, Dutch authorities are portrayed as responding to a spontaneous demand for intervention not just from one of the parties in a local conflict, but from both or all of them.²⁵ While treaties between the VOC and its vas-

---

23 The Dutch naval captain Van der Hart (1853: 244), circumnavigating Sulawesi in 1850, concluded that the Bugis were effectively 'masters of all the trade in these regions'. Sutherland (1995: 138-40) discusses the superiority of Bugis and Chinese traders over their Dutch rivals in Sulawesi during the 18th and 19th centuries.
24 AR Gorontalo to Res. Manado, 20.9.1827 (ANRI Manado 114).
25 Examples in published documents: Buddingh 1860: 345; CD III: 109; V: 51, 61, 63-4, 130, 446-7, 569, 578, 597; GM VI: 349; IX: 677; XI: 512; Godée Molsbergen 1928: 64, 132; Watuseke and Henley 1994: 371-2.

While inland villages were mostly built on hilltops and integrally fortified, the typical coastal settlement was located close to a 'refuge hill' (vluchtberg) with a fortified outpost to which its inhabitants could flee in the event of an attack. This illustration shows Sawang (Greater Sangir) and its vluchtberg as sketched from a VOC ship in 1679. Source: ARA VOC 1345:867.

sals or allies often stipulated that serious conflicts were to be submitted to Company officials for arbitration (Alders 1955: 122-6), the number and apparent triviality of the disputes which these men were asked to resolve surprised and sometimes irritated them.[26] In some cases the primary function of Dutch mediation

26 In 1804, for instance, one resident of Manado wrote that 'this residency gives much more work than any other in the Moluccas because of its size and the many complaints [conflicts] which occur every day, all of which have to be decided by the resident himself' (Watuseke and Henley 1994: 366). In Roti (eastern Nusa Tenggara), likewise, the VOC found it impossible 'not to become involved in the interminable squabbles of the Rotinese' as local leaders 'were able to seize upon the new modes of adjudication that the Dutch offered in order to promote their own ends' (Fox 1977: 82).

was to guarantee the peace during negotiations between embittered enemies: in 1863, for instance, the scientist Von Rosenberg (1865: 47), visiting Central Sulawesi in an armed government sailing vessel, claimed to have prevented war between two groups which had sought his intervention simply by arranging a peace conference 'on the seashore under the cannon of the patrol boat'.[27] More often, however, such mediation took a more active form involving the provision of formal adjudication by the Dutch themselves. In 1686, the VOC outpost in Manado was already playing a thoroughly institutionalised judicial role not only for the population of its immediate Minahasan hinterland, but also for that of the Sangir islands some 200 km to its north.

> 'Our experience is that the occupation of Manado is of greater importance than some perhaps believe, in that it enables the Governor [of Ternate], who is not always able to make extensive journeys himself, as well as His Excellency [the governor-general], to be completely confident that no disorder or difficulties will arise on the [Sangir] islands. For it is well known that nearly all the petty kings and nobles of those islands frequently arrive in Manado to have their disputes resolved by the fair, modest, and impartial judgement of the commander there, whereafter the disputants return home in peace. Although such disputes are mostly of little importance, they are hereby prevented from assuming more dangerous forms. And this is to say nothing of the differences which almost continuously arise between the Manadonese [Minahasan] chiefs and villagers, and which, if not quickly settled, lead to confusion, chaos, petty local wars, and bloodshed.' (ARA VOC 1428: 170r).

Three years later, the Dutch commander in Manado even opined that the Sangirese kings 'cannot govern their own lands and villages, still less resolve their mutual differences, without the authority, intervention, and assistance of the Honourable Company, which they constantly seek to invoke not only as mediator or referee, but also as their highest judge [*opperrigter*]' (ARA VOC 1461: 478r). By the beginning of the nineteenth century, Dutch dispute adjudication in Minahasa itself had assumed a routinised, even ritualised form in which the resident was assisted by a judicial committee comprising the heads of the seven indigenous quarters (*walak*) of Manado town, but always had to be represented by a symbol of his personal authority.

---

27 This pattern was a traditional one; in parts of upland Luzon (Philippines), comparably, conflict mediators were traditionally 'honor bound to punish infractions of the peace by either side while mediation is in process with death or wounding' (Barton 1949: 164).

'Whenever a dispute arising in one of the vassal districts is too serious to be resolved locally, or the chiefs cannot reach an agreement among themselves (which is invariably the case), the issue is brought before the resident, who settles it in consultation with the seven *walak* immediately surrounding this fort. Alternatively the resident sends a representative, accompanied by the deputy chiefs of the same seven villages, to investigate and resolve the case. These take with them a large staff with a silver head bearing the Company coat of arms, and when people see this they regard it as almost as good as if the resident had come in person. The natives, however, seldom wait so long, but instead come to the resident themselves because they know that he is impartial, which is not usually true of his representatives.' (C.C. Prediger, Verhandeling Manado 1804, in Watuseke and Henley 1994: 371-2).

Here the resident is explicitly preferred above indigenous arbitrators not in the first place because he is the highest or most powerful judge, but because of his reputation for impartiality. Dutch dispute resolution during the VOC period was in fact less effective than this rather smug account would suggest, for tribal wars continued sporadically in Minahasa up to 1809. The most severe, however, resulted precisely from abortive Dutch attempts to reduce expenses by delegating judicial authority to indigenous go-betweens: on three occasions during the eighteenth century, particular Minahasan chiefs were granted special powers which they immediately employed to favour their own kin groups, thereby attracting the jealousy and anger of their peers and making their position untenable (Henley 1996: 36-7; Schouten 1998: 44-5). There is little reason to doubt that the more direct and even-handed conflict management provided by the Dutch under normal circumstances was an important element of the remarkable symbiosis which developed between the Minahasans and the *kumpania*, as they called both the VOC and the colonial state, over a period of 150 years. So completely were the Dutch incorporated into the 'traditional' political system that by 1804 the people of Minahasa could be described as 'very much attached to ancient customs, and to the Company, [mention of] the word Company being sufficient to make them do almost anything' (Watuseke and Henley 1994: 376).

If we see the foreign state partly as an instrument by which Minahasans sought to organise their own society, then it also becomes easier to understand why over time the insignia and terminology of Dutch government, rather than coming to be seen as symbols of foreign oppression, became symbols of cooperation among local people themselves. An important feature of Minahasan economic life in the nineteenth and early twentieth centuries was *mapalus*, an institution of reciprocal labour exchange in which large groups of farmers, sometimes up to 100 at a time, took turns to perform such tasks as scrub clearance, planting and weeding on each others' fields.[28] *Mapalus* was an unusually corporate and harshly disciplined variant of what Indonesians now call *gotong-royong* (Bowen 1986; Koentjaraningrat 1961). It featured elected leaders who administered punishment in the form of whiplashes to individuals whose work tempo fell behind that of the others, but who at the time of their appointment were themselves ceremonially lashed by each member in order to preserve the egalitarian, reciprocal character of the institution. The banner of every large *mapalus* corporation, around which its members assembled before setting out for the fields and which they planted on the particular piece of land to be worked, was a Dutch flag. The individual names given to the corporations (Graafland 1864: 12) included 'Resident', 'Governor-General', and '*korakora*' (a type of Moluccan seacraft employed by the Dutch to defend the Minahasan coasts against pirates). The internal organisation of some *mapalus* groups was also derived partly from Dutch models:

> 'The leaders are often given the titles of government officials: 'resident', 'fiscal', '*jaksa* [public prosecutor]', '*oppas* [supervisor]', '*pion* [messenger]' and so on. The '*jaksa*' investigates any disputes which arise and the 'resident' imposes sentences, which are implemented by the 'supervisors' or strongmen among them. These sentences often take the form of corporal punishment.' (A.H.D. Supit 1929: 4.)

How much the substance of the *mapalus* as an institution actually owed to foreign inspiration is not entirely clear; the symbolism surrounding it, however, reflects a strong perceived association between the institutions of foreign government and the promotion of effective collective action even in the absence of government officials themselves.[29]

The equation of leadership with law was no innovation of the colonial period, but had deep roots in indigenous society. The single most important function of most traditional leaders in northern Sulawesi was neither military nor economic, but judicial.[30] A large proportion of the income of such leaders came

---

28 Hekker (1987: 108-14) provides an overview of the literature on this and related forms of *mapalus*; the earliest description dates from 1825. The following sources are particularly significant with respect to the points to be mentioned above: Beck 1922; Graafland 1864: 10-13; A.H.D. Supit 1929.

29 In the mid-19th century, so-called *mapalus* groups were sometimes organised under state auspices for the performance of corvée labour (Edeling 1919: 55); the descriptions cited above, however, do not refer to these.

30 Christine Dobbin (1975: 78) and Barbara Andaya (1993: 31) have come to the same conclusion with respect to various Sumatran *raja*, and Fox (1977: 82) states that for the Rotinese the 'essential feature' of a state is a (law) court.

from the share which they received in the fines which they imposed when disputes between two or more of their followers were brought before them, almost always on a voluntary basis by the disputants themselves, for arbitration.³¹ 'All legitimate political authorities', observed the anthropologist Thomas Kiefer (1972: 86) among the Tausug of Jolo in the nearby Sulu archipelago during the 1960s, were 'regarded primarily as juridical officials'. In fact the Tausug term for 'law', *sara* (from Arabic *shari'a*), was 'used to collectively describe all headmen in Jolo, from the weakest headman up to the sultan himself' (Kiefer 1972: 88). Until well into the nineteenth century, likewise, the Malay word *hukum*—again an Arabic borrowing literally meaning 'law', but often translated in Dutch documents as *rechter* or 'judge' (Malay: *hakim*)—served as a generic term for chiefs of diverse descriptions throughout North Sulawesi and the North Moluccas.³² Judicial and executive powers, of course, were not distinct, and in order to become such a judge it was usually necessary to demonstrate, among other things, military prowess. The Dutch were not exempt from this requirement: 'I do not believe', lamented Albert Kruyt in Central Sulawesi shortly before its conquest, 'that the government will acquire any important influence [here] until it has fought with one or other [indigenous] people' (J. Kruyt 1970: 94). The quality of the justice which a leader could offer, nevertheless, was also an important criterion of his fitness for leadership.³³

---

31 Aragon 1992: 54; Godée Molsbergen 1928: 189; Goedhart 1908: 460; Hissink 1912: 99; A.C. Kruyt 1932: 341; 1938, I: 524; *Landschap Donggala* 1905: 525; Riedel 1872: 512; Steller 1866: 27; Watuseke and Henley 1994: 370-71.
32 Watuseke 1986: 320. The distribution of this term probably reflects the intermediate role of the sultanate of Ternate, which enjoyed political suzerainty over North Sulawesi during the late 16th and early 17th centuries (Henley 1993: 56). There is little doubt, however, that its users were aware of its legal and judicial connotations (also: W.H. Scott 1994: 139).
33 As criteria of selection for the rank of *pangat* or chief (also called 'peacemaker' and 'right-determiner') among the Kalinga of upland Luzon, comparably, Barton (1949: 148) lists 'fairness (meaning suprakinship vision)' alongside wealth, lineage, oratorical ability, and 'a reputation as a dangerous man'.

4 The problem of jealousy

In northern Sulawesi, the need for effective conflict resolution was made all the more pressing by the intensely competitive character of the local societies. These were not in any straightforward sense egalitarian; slavery, for instance, was an almost universal institution, and the 'vertical orientation' characteristic of Southeast Asian social life (Reid 1983: 6-8) was everywhere strongly evident.[34] Social mobility, however, was also pronounced, individuals and kin groups struggling constantly to improve their position by achieving success in agriculture or war, by attaching themselves to influential patrons, or by otherwise accumulating enough resources to hold potlatch-like, status-boosting feasts of merit (Schouten 1998: 22-38; Schrauwers 2000: 68-70). No non-slave could easily be excluded from political decision-making, the process of which often struck European observers as both democratic and cumbersome:

> 'There are so many interests to be considered [...] that people must deliberate long and carefully before they can come to a [collective] decision. They take each others' interests into account because they are afraid of each another; somebody whose interests have been damaged sets his heart on revenge [...]. For this reason they are on their guard against one another, and in matters involving a large number of people it often happened that no decision could be taken because nobody dared to accept the necessary responsibility.' (Adriani and Kruyt 1950-51, I: 114.)

---

34 Slave status, besides being hereditable, could be acquired as a result of debt, crime, or capture in war; slaves, conversely, could often purchase their freedom. General descriptions of slavery in various parts of northern Sulawesi are given by Hissink (1912: 107-10), A.C. Kruyt (1911; 1938, I: 512-21), Schouten (1998: 31-2) and Steller (1866: 40-44).

If there was a single underlying reason for the scarcity of political centralisation or deep, stable social hierarchy, it was probably the scarcity of structural opportunities for aspiring elites to secure exclusive access to valuable economic resources. In a region which produced few valuable trade products, where there were no large navigable rivers, and where no place lay more than 90 kilometres from the sea, there were few of those natural 'choke points' or bottlenecks of commerce which Scott (1998a: 53) calls 'potential state spaces'. The more immediate, routine obstacle to the establishment of secure economic and social privileges, however, was jealous competition for wealth, status, and the allegiance of the lower orders. Padtbrugge (1866: 310) already noted that the Minahasans were 'very jealous [naijverig] of each other', and Schouten (1988) once chose the title 'Eternal rivalry' for a popular article describing Minahasan culture through the centuries. In 1949 the last Dutch resident of Manado described the divisive effect of this rivalry as a 'Minahasan fission fungus [splijtzwam]' undermining every local attempt to form effective political organisations.[35] 'All these islanders', observed the adventurer Cuarteron (1855: 103) during a sojourn in Sangir and Talaud in 1848, 'are extremely avaricious, proud, ambitious, and envious of one another'; after fieldwork on Siau in 1952-53 the anthropologist Hendrik Chabot (1969: 95), better known for his earlier work on the notoriously competitive Bugis and Makasar peoples of South Sulawesi, declared that he had 'seldom lived among people who to me seemed so inharmonious'.

To some extent, the endemic warfare which prevailed in most parts of the region prior to European intervention was simply one manifestation of status competition; in Central Sulawesi, reportedly, jealousy (especially of material wealth) was in itself a common reason for going to war.[36] The same sentiment, interestingly, was also involved in the custom of hunting enemy heads in connection with the funeral ceremonies of prominent people. Dutch observers tended to assume that this practice had to do either with a belief that the victims would serve the deceased as slaves in the afterlife, or with revenge for a death which the headhunters had interpreted as a murder by magical means. When questioned on the subject, however, indigenous informants offered only partial support for either of these views, and in Minahasa the *controleur* F.S.A. de Clercq, generally a careful and rather sympathetic observer of local culture, recorded a quite different explanation for the link between bereavement and headhunting.[37]

---

35 Halfmaandelijks politiek-economisch verslag Manado, 1-15.7.1949 (ARA ASB I.X.2.8). Also: Harvey 1977: 122; Henley 1996: 112.
36 A.C. Kruyt 1938, II: 56; Kruyt and Kruyt 1921: 407. Compare: Barton 1938: 131.
37 A similar statement was recorded in Central Sulawesi by Albert Kruyt (1938, III: 491). This interpretation is broadly congruent with the 'emotional' analysis of Ilongot headhunting presented by Renato Rosaldo (1980: 140).

'[Headhunts] occurred mainly on the death of certain individuals, when another person always had to be killed and his skull (*takin*), after his blood had been drunk from it, hung up in the vicinity of the grave. [...] In no way was revenge the underlying motive here; this was done only in order to comfort the blood relatives of the deceased, who no longer had to bear their pain alone now that others too had been plunged into grief by the loss of one of their kin.' (De Clercq 1870b: 5).

In the 1920s a colonial schools inspector, noting the jealousy with which Minahasan villagers responded to any advantage in terms of school facilities enjoyed by their neighbours, quipped that the slogan *Waarom ik niet?* 'should have been inscribed in the Minahasan coat of arms' (De Nes 1925: 503). In earlier times, it seems, the principle of 'Why not me?' as applied to the good things in life also had a sinister correlate when it came to experiences of pain and loss: 'Why not you?'.[38]

It is not clear to what degree the pervading spirit of jealousy was itself a by-product of the hostile relations which typically prevailed between neighbouring groups, or whether it was more closely associated with levelling mechanisms which served to promote political and economic solidarity within individual communities (Miller and Cook 1998: 72-82; Sahlins 1972: 87-8). But whatever its causes, its consequences in the political sphere were far-reaching. By making it difficult for any indigenous leader to generate much genuine loyalty, for instance, local jealousies greatly facilitated colonial rule. Minahasans were always well known for making 'passionate complaints' (AV Manado 1853, in ANRI Manado 51) against their own leaders, and in 1829 a Dutch resident of Manado noted that the dismissal of an insubordinate Minahasan chief, far from resulting in political unrest, could typically be accomplished 'without the least fear of unpleasant consequences, and even to the satisfaction [*genoegen*] of the lesser chiefs' (AV Manado 1829, in KITLV H70).[39] The Dutch themselves, standing largely outside the society and rivalries of the chiefs, were relatively immune from attempts at jealous subversion, and under most circumstances their authority was more acceptable to any single Minahasan leader than was that of any of his

---

38 One of the reasons why the dead had to be propitiated with sacrifices, tellingly, was that they were assumed to be destructively jealous of the living (Woensdregt 1928: 223).
39 After literacy became widespread as a result of mission education in the course of the 19th century, Minahasans constantly sought Dutch help in their efforts to undermine their superiors by submitting written complaints about them to the colonial authorities (Fragment 1856: 93; Gallois 1892: 3; De Nes 1925: 501).
40 The same factor was later to facilitate colonial rule in the highlands of North Sumatra, where the form of authority most likely to generate resentment among Bataks was that of a fellow Batak (Angerler 1995: 138).

peers.⁴⁰ So effective was this political compromise that in the pseudo-colonial symbolism of *mapalus*, we can arguably see an attempt to pretend that Dutch authority was in force even when it was not. At another level, the jealousy with which individuals and kin groups reacted to any attempt by their peers to disadvantage them also tended to put third-party mediators, whether indigenous or foreign, in a very strong position. A description of conflict ajudication on the Sangir islands, written by a visiting colonial official in 1825, provides a neat metaphor for the way in which such behaviour facilitated the expansion of foreign power with the compliance of the indigenous population. 'Both parties', this source states, 'would rather see everything surrendered to the judges, who are thereby recompensed for their trouble, than that either one of them should give up his own pretended rights to it' (Van Delden 1844: 378).

5 The problem of justice

These, then, were litigatious societies in which the need for judicial authority, and indeed justice, was deeply felt.[41] Yet they were also small-scale, stateless societies in which kin solidarity and gift exchange, both principles inherently inconsistent with the impartial administration of justice, were the very basis of the political order, and within which it was consequently difficult to find individuals whose judgement in any given dispute was likely to be unprejudiced.[42] One solution was to choose an arbitrator whose blood ties with both parties were equally strong (Adriani 1916: 114), and village heads, the most common choices for this purpose, often owed their rank partly to the way in which their genealogies united the various corporate kin groups (typically diffuse matrilineages) present in their communities. Another common approach, however, was to seek the involvement of outsiders.[43] In his description of seventeenth-century Minahasa, Padtbrugge (1866: 315) already noted that 'minor and civil disputes' be-

---

41 Adriani 1916: 116; Adriani and Kruyt 1912-14, II: 168; A.C. Kruyt 1908: 1314-15; Padtbrugge 1866: 313, 315.
42 Adriani 1916: 114; 1932: 48-9; Frieswijck 1902: 374; Riedel 1872: 227. Toward the end of a 400-page treatise on the customary law of the Toba Batak, the colonial legal expert J.C. Vergouwen (1964: 388-9) conceded that there was a fundamental problem with the administration of that law: 'the Batak do not in general possess in their chiefs judges who are unselfish, impartial and incorruptible'. The Batak judge, in his experience, was both 'susceptible to bribery' and 'seldom capable of being competely impartial if one of the parties is a somewhat close kinsman or affine of his'.
43 Adriani and Kruyt 1950-51, I: 118; A.C. Kruyt 1938, II: 217; Ter Laag 1920: 38. Among the Kalinga of Luzon, noted Barton (1949: 164), a 'go-between' or arbitrator 'should preferably be related to both sides in the dispute or else to neither'.

tween co-villagers were customarily resolved 'not in the [home] village itself, but in another, where they believe these can be judged better, and without any bias [*buiten alle eenzijdigheid*]'. Under favourable circumstances, the same procedure could even be used to end inter-village wars:

> 'When both sides have suffered too much either in open war or from repeated headhunting raids, or neighbouring groups begin to be affected or fear that the conflict will escalate, some people from neutral villages visit both parties and begin to calm their emotions. A peace-loving person is then appointed who listens to the story from both sides and reconciles the opposing chiefs in such a way that the guilty one must pay a fine, consisting mostly of brassware, gongs, arm rings, slaves and suchlike, commensurate with the estimated wealth of his village.' (Padtbrugge 1866: 319.)

Given that intermarriage did occur between villages and village confederacies, on the other hand, local 'outsiders' like these were seldom completely immune from accusations of bias, and often risked being drawn into the conflict themselves; the memory of past blood feuds, always carefully preserved in oral tradition, also complicated their task.[44] A more radical solution was to rely on the more impartial arbitration of a more complete outsider—preferably one who was also wealthy enough to be relatively immune from bribery, and powerful enough in military terms to take on either one of the warring parties (not necessarily both of them combined) should it refuse, after the event, to accept his verdict.

In the interior of Central Sulawesi before the colonial conquest this alien third party was often the *raja*, typically a man of Bugis descent, at the head of one of the coastal trading polities to which the upland or 'Toraja' population professed formal allegiance (*mepue*).[45] 'People say', recorded Kruyt (1938, I: 177), 'that the advantage of this *mepue* lay in the fact that because the ruler now came between the opposing parties in all kinds of conflicts, the tribes were no longer free to fine and attack each other arbitrarily'. Of course the peacemaking 'service' provided by the *raja*, as Schrauwers (1997: 372-3) has recently emphasised, was seldom offered on a disinterested basis. For the paramount *mokole* (*raja*) of

---

[44] Padtbrugge 1866: 316-7. A later VOC source notes that Minahasans reckon their kin 'to 20 degrees and more', and that the murder of any of these leads to 'eternal conflict, especially since the barbaric custom of displaying the heads, arms, and legs of slaughtered enemies in front of their houses, and making necklaces from their teeth, always provides fresh reason to reopen old wounds' (Godée Molsbergen 1928: 101).

[45] Technically obsolete except as an ethnonym for the Sa'dang people of upland South Sulawesi, the term Toraja is used here for convenience in its older sense as a general designation for the ethnically diverse pagan upland populations of Central Sulawesi.

Mori in eastern Central Sulawesi, for instance, arbitration often formed only one part of a broader political strategy in which upland divisions were also exploited by more violent and less impartial means.

> 'Every new conflict provides an opportunity for the *mokole* to increase his influence. For when neither party voluntarily comes to him for support, he will offer to mediate an amicable settlement. If both parties decline this offer, then he must wait for a more favourable moment. But as a rule one of the parties will be prepared to accept the offer; if the other then rejects the interference of the *mokole*, the latter will enter the fray on the side of the one who was prepared to accept his services.' (J. Kruyt 1924: 56.)

Viewed like this, conflict mediation seems a transparent veil for imperialism. From the standpoint of the combatants, on the other hand, the same strategy looked decidedly less sinister, and in fact the readiness of the king to offer his arbitration spontaneously, rather than only on request, could be a positive windfall.

> 'The normal procedure was [...] that a neutral chief brought about the armistice. [...] This, of course, had to be a chief with power and influence. Occasionally such a man offered spontaneously to make peace; in that case he had to bear all of the costs involved himself, because both parties always pretended to be outraged that somebody was coming between them, even if in their hearts they were delighted that peace would be restored. Each was obliged to behave as if it would rather fight on; neither could countenance the thought of having been defeated. Usually, however, a neutral chief only took steps to make peace after one or both parties had requested him to do so out of a feeling that the war could not be kept up any longer.' (A.C. Kruyt 1938, II: 217-18.)

In Minahasa, where the Dutch were the apical mediators, their incentive to pursue an even-handed policy of judicial pacification was strengthened by the fact that any conflict quickly tended to interfere with the production and supply of the Minahasan rice which, purchased using Indian textiles, formed the Company's main economic interest in the area (Schouten 1998: 42-3, 50). While the Dutch always attempted to force down prices by soliciting political trading privileges and suppressing competition, they were equally concerned to ensure the security and continuity of that commerce which they already controlled. To quote Robert Padtbrugge again:

> 'They fight with each other over nothing, and war, once ignited, spreads through the villages like a bush fire. Each man chooses sides according to his

own notions or interests, or simply with a view to obtaining heads, even those of old men and women or innocent children. When such a fire breaks out we immediately send some of our own people, preferably those with knowledge of the local customs and languages, to douse it. Because the advice and judgements of the Company are regarded here as oracles [*Godsspraken*], even serious conflicts can be resolved by their mediation [...]' (Godée Molsbergen 1928: 63-4.)

Where such human 'oracles' were unavailable or unable to give a clear verdict, another option (particularly in disputes not involving homicide) was to turn to the real thing, usually in the form of a competitive ordeal by water (immersion) or fire for both parties or their champions, the result of which was regarded as a supernatural judgement.[46] As in the case of arbitration by foreigners, an important consideration here was that no insider had to take responsibility for a mistaken, resented, or contested decision. 'Wise Torajas', noted Adriani (1915: 472), 'do recognise that innocent people have often been condemned as a result of a divine trial [*godsoordeel*], but responsibility for this was borne by the gods, and the issue was at least settled once and for all'.[47] By the same logic, the Toraja were sometimes happy to leave the execution of a criminal to outsiders in order to avoid the risk of internal vengeance killings by his kinsmen. The hated To Napu, for instance, were reportedly often called in by their enemies 'to get rid of somebody whose impossible behaviour had made him persona non grata among his fellow tribesmen' (A.C. Kruyt 1938, I: 257).[48]

Dutch officials admitted that they did not always understand the details of the indigenous conflicts which they were asked to adjudicate (Godée Molsbergen 1928: 64; Watuseke and Henley 1994: 376), and it might be assumed that their ignorance of customary law was a great obstacle to their acceptance as judges; certainly they were often obliged to rely heavily on their interpreters, and on the lowland chiefs of Manado, for advice. In some cases, however, the unpredictability and inscrutability of Dutch adjudication may actually have been a point in its favour, for disinterested ignorance was probably preferable in an arbitrator to anything which could be interpreted as knowledgeable manipulation. Chance,

---

46 Adriani 1932: 41-4; Frieswijck 1902: 475; Padtbrugge 1866: 316; *Tooe oen Boeloesch ordalium* 1864. Very similar procedures, of course, were once common in Europe (Tewksbury 1967).
47 War itself, the outcome of which 'was interpreted entirely as a divine judgement' (Adriani 1921: 19), can be viewed as a still higher court of appeal in the same hierarchy of divine jurisdiction.
48 Here I was reminded of an episode in the autobiography of a celebrated European stranger-king, T.E. Lawrence (of Arabia). At least according to his own account, Lawrence was once able to preserve the unity of an Arab force by executing a murderer whose killing by another Arab would have precipitated an outbreak of feuding. 'At least no revenge could lie against my followers', he noted, 'for I was a stranger and kinless' (Lawrence 1935: 181).

after all, has its own kind of objectivity, and nothing is more impartial than a lottery (Elster 1989: 36-122). Here again there is a parallel with divine or magic oracles: Evans-Pritchard (1976: 158), in his classic study of these devices in an African context, described how the Azande tested their poison oracle (poison fed to chickens which might either die or survive) to make sure it was producing something approaching a random sequence of verdicts before actually consulting it for a judgement or prophesy. Just as the most authoritative oracles among the Azande were controlled by princes, nobles in Central Sulawesi adjudicated the most difficult of the disputes brought before them with the aid of trials by ordeal which only they had the right to stage (A.C. Kruyt 1932b: 254-5; J. Kruyt 1924: 97-8). In peninsular North Sulawesi, some myths (of which more below) regarding indigenous kingship portrayed the *raja* not as wise or rational men but as 'children, to whom all power and pomp are surrendered simply to play with' (Van Wouden 1941: 378).

The judicial function of the state was not so indispensable that people were immediately prepared to accept heavy taxation or far-reaching trade monopolies for its sake alone. More typically, upland populations attempted to balance the benefits and burdens of interaction with the coastal *raja* by settling just far enough away from them to minimise their fiscal impositions while still taking advantage of their judicial (and commercial) services. Reid (1997: 80-81) has proposed that tribal populations deliberately isolated themselves in the interior of the larger Indonesian islands in order to preserve their independence, and Adriani (1919: 5-6) wrote in a similar vein that the uninhabited 'forest girdle' surrounding the Toraja uplands of Central Sulawesi had been left intact 'as a barrier between their territory and that of the coastal people'. With a typical breadth of just a few hours' walk, however, this 'barrier' was very far from being impenetrable, and its existence might even be interpreted partly as a functional consequence of the particular type of political interaction wich existed between the stateless uplands and the lowland polities. In order to continue playing their judicial role effectively, the *raja* had to remain permanent outsiders and could not be allowed to become integral members of the community; one obvious way of preventing this was to keep them at a geographical distance.

6 Warfare, ritual, and collective action

The extent to which the prevalence of conflict and violence reflected nothing more the 'natural' chaos of the stateless condition, of course, must not be exaggerated. As in other parts of Southeast Asia, warfare in precolonial Sulawesi was underpinned not only by hereditary feuds and the weakness of state authority, but also by competition for economic resources such as high-quality agricultural land and slave labour, and by the cultural factors which one seventeenth-century VOC official in Manado summed up as 'the well-known honour which the uplanders [berg-boeren] see in killing people and proudly displaying their severed heads' (ARA VOC 1461: 488r-v).[49] A powerful complex of beliefs and rituals, in fact, linked bravery and bloodshed at a supernatural level with welfare and prosperity as well as honour and renown.

> 'The Toraja of Central Sulawesi, in the ideal state of their society, would have been a people of [warrior-]heroes and priestesses. It was the men in their role as headhunters, and the women as priestesses, who brought back the booty of health and longevity to the members of their tribe from outside its territory. To this end they made long and dangerous journeys: the headhunters to the hostile regions of this Middle World, the priestesses to the Upper- or Underworld.' (Adriani 1917: 453).

---

49 The relevance of territory as an economic resource in Southeast Asian tribal societies is often underestimated; in areas of high agricultural value such as the central plateau of Minahasa, boundary disputes were common causes of conflict (Godée Molsbergen 1928: 132; Watuseke and Henley 1994: 378).

At the same time, nevertheless, there was also a sense in which violence, like lesser forms of conflict, was perceived as a problem rather than a necessity, and foreign intervention as a solution to that problem. After the colonial conquest of Central Sulawesi in the years 1905-7, the once-proud (and still pagan) Toraja warriors, while deeply resentful of corvée labour demands and many other aspects of Dutch rule, reportedly found the prohibition of headhunting 'fair [*billijk*], since they understood that the *kumpania* [the Dutch government] was fully capable of maintaining the peace' (Adriani 1915: 471). The sacral logic of war, moreover, did not prove a serious obstacle to the enforcement of that peace; domestic warfare in Central Sulawesi ceased almost immediately following the Dutch conquest.[50] This was an outcome which Adriani and Kruyt, convinced that beneath their self-consciously warlike veneer Toraja people were essentially 'gentle, peace-loving and timorous by nature' (A.C. Kruyt 1938, II: 55), had already predicted before the pacification.[51]

> 'If they had a valid excuse to offer to the ancestors, then they would be absolved. If one or another power which the Toraja feared were expressly to prohibit them from hunting heads, then after the rice harvest when the annual raiding season began those who had not yet ended their mourning for a deceased relative, and were therefore obliged to participate this time, would solemnly declare to the souls of their dead that they would have been pleased to perform a headhunt if [...] the *kumpania* had not forbidden it. [...] [I]f the prohibition is rigorously enforced, then they will abandon headhunting and learn, just as the Minahasans have already learned, the natural abhorrence of this murderous practice which is at present suppressed by the cruelty of experience.' (Adriani 1901b: 247-8.)

The end of headhunting, although it occurred with remarkable speed, was no doubt more of a cultural trauma than this passage implies, and in fact helped pave the way (as the missionaries had hoped it would) for the conversion of the Toraja to Christianity from 1909 onward (J. Kruyt 1970: 106-18). It should also be noted that in the new unfortified villages in which they were forcibly resettled after the conquest, the Toraja were forbidden to build the *lobo* or 'temples' in which trophy skulls had formerly been preserved and headhunting ceremonies held (Adriani 1915: 469). The fact that pacification preceded religious change rather than vice versa, nevertheless, is consistent with the Hobbesian view that it

---

50 A last (failed) headhunt was reported from Parigi in 1914 (KV 1915: 35).
51 It is perhaps worth noting in this context that before a raid, Toraja headhunters often ate hallucinogenic mushrooms in order to make themselves 'insensitive to all danger' (A.C. Kruyt 1899: 157).

was the circumstance of statelessness itself, more than the particular beliefs of the stateless peoples, which had previously perpetuated the condition of Warre.

Eighty years earlier it had been a similar story in Minahasa, where the Christianisation of the upland population from 1831 onward (Henley 1996: 52-3) also followed, rather than preceded, military pacification. The Tondano War of 1808-9, in which the colonial government deployed European, Moluccan and local troops in an unprecedented (and in Minahasa never again equalled) demonstration of its power, marked not only the definitive defeat of anticolonial resistance in the area, but also the end of domestic warfare on any scale among Minahasans themselves.[52] In the space of a few years, the inhabitants were transformed in contemporary Dutch accounts from bloodthirsty (if ingenuous) savages into model subjects whose 'good and peaceful nature' made it possible to maintain peace and order throughout Minahasa with the help of just six policemen (AV Manado 1824, in ANRI Manado 101). Here again, the suppression of war as such was also accompanied by a more or less specific attack on its ritual aspects: at some point between 1812 and 1815, all trophy heads which could be found in Minahasa were brought to the fort in Manado and burned (Roorda van Eysinga 1831: 106). A decade later, nevertheless, resident Johannes Wenzel insisted that only a lack of 'firm government' had been to blame for the internecine violence of former times:

> 'It was a mistake to assume that the people were bloodthirsty, or to believe that the killing was a consequence of their [religious] feasts. Many feasts were consequences of killing; even today it is a general custom that when the native experiences some misfortune, or has committed some act which his instinct tells him was wrong, he promises to hold a *foso* or feast if fate should extract him from his unpleasant circumstance. [...] It was mistaken, I repeat, to portray the native as bloodthirsty; wars between the districts, which had their origins in a lack of firm government, were viewed as episodes of assassination, and the defence of property as violent aggression.' (Riedel 1872 [1825]: 513-4.)

In Minahasa as in Central Sulawesi, then, a short period of rigorous peace enforcement seems to have been enough to jerk a whole political system from one stable equilibrium of self-perpetuating violence into another of largely self-sus-

---

52 By 1822, according to one contemporary source, the custom of headhunting had already 'fallen completely into disuse' (Roorda van Eysinga 1831: 106). Occasional headhunts, however, did in fact continue in secret after this date (Graafland 1867-69, I: 128, 286-7; Pietermaat, De Vriese and Lucas 1840: 130), the last on record taking place as late as 1862 (De Clercq 1870b: 5).

taining peace. Although fear of the state's proven coercive power remained a significant element of the new order (Adriani 1919: 188; Graafland 1867-69, I: 273), the actual use of military force seldom or never had to be repeated once an armistice was imposed, the cycle of revenge broken, and beliefs in the cosmic necessity of violence undermined by the experience of peace. The problem of jealousy, of course, remained, but now people had much more to lose by translating envy into violence and risking not only punishment by the state, but also a resumption of reciprocal feuding. As a reputation for vengefulness became less and less of a practical necessity for the purpose of defending kin and property, meanwhile, the way also opened up for ethical changes, reinforced in the Minahasan and Toraja cases by conversion to Christianity, which began to undermine even the emotional roots of conflict.[53]

In the days before the colonial state had conclusively demonstrated what Hobbes (see p. 7 above) would have called the 'Power to keep them in awe', few people were humble, altruistic, or indeed irrational enough to give up the right to revenge without any solid guarantee that their enemies would do the same. In this period the problem of violence, whatever its cultural and religious underpinnings, also tended to take the form of what game theorists call a 'collective action dilemma': even if all parties agreed that a lasting peace would be to their mutual advantage, none could refrain from taking violent revenge for past injuries without conveying 'a timidity which invited further enemy action' (W.H. Scott 1994: 153).[54] Under such circumstances the best that could be hoped for was the negotiation of an armed truce when a particular conflict lasted too long or threatened to get out of hand. Here again, however, the Dutch state already came in useful, for while no military Leviathan as yet, it was often already capable of facing down individual players in the indigenous power game provided the others remained neutral or supportive. Equally important, it also met another criterion identified by Hobbes (1996: 109) as desirable in a peacemaking author-

---

[53] The logic of vengeance under stateless conditions is well expressed by John Crawfurd's admission, in his *History of the Indian Archipelago* (1820, I: 65), that 'where the security of every man's honour, life, and property, depends in no small degree upon his own arm, we may almost hesitate whether to pronounce the passion of revenge a virtue or a vice'.

[54] Lichbach (1996) summarises the immense game-theoretical literature on problems of rationality and cooperation. Readers familiar with this literature may wonder why, other than for cultural reasons, relations between neighbouring groups so often settled into the 'negative reciprocity' (Sahlins 1965: 91) of feuding rather than the positive reciprocity of 'live and let live' (Axelrod 1990). One was that the parties in any given conflict seldom agreed on who had started it, so that what was justified retaliation to one was an unprovoked attack to another (Barton 1969: 69; Poundstone 1992: 254). Another was that wars tended to involve more than two parties, so that instead of being a relatively simple matter of bilateral reciprocity, peace acquired the more elusive quality of a public good (Molander 1992).

ity: as long as its vassals all continued to meet their contractual trading obligations, it was not in general a judge 'to whom greater profit, or honour, or pleasure apparently ariseth out of the victory of one party, than of the other'. The status of the Dutch as ethnic, genealogical, and social outsiders, in other words, gave their arbitration a degree of objectivity and impartiality which could seldom be hoped for from any existing indigenous authority.[55]

---

55 Here again, we are reminded of parallels with trading minorities. The 'objectivity' which the 'stranger' is able to bring to trade relations, according to Georg Simmel's classic thesis, is one of his key commercial advantages (Simmel 1908: 685-91).

7 The rebel's dilemma

All this is not to suggest that anticolonial resistance never occurred, or even that an ideal of collective political freedom, as identified by Reid (1998a: 145-9) in some other parts of precolonial Indonesia, was never present. At the beginning of the nineteenth century, relations between the Minahasans and the Dutch government became increasingly strained following a decline in the price paid by the state for Minahasan rice, the imposition of an unpaid rice levy to finance the (never very effective) defence of the Minahasan coasts against slave raiders, and finally a clumsy attempt to recruit 2,000 men as soldiers to help defend Java against the British. In June 1808, chiefs (hukum) from almost all of the major Minahasan village federations (walak) gathered in Tondano to swear a formal oath, sealed in the traditional manner by stepping over crossed weapons (Riedel 1864b), by which they severed all relations with the Dutch and effectively declared war on the government.[56] Participants later remembered that Minahasa as a whole had 'wished to be free' from the kumpania (Graafland 1867-69, I: 285), and described the oath as reflecting a 'general desire for liberation' (Mangindaän 1873: 367).

This aspiration, it has been noted, was ultimately thwarted by defeat at the hands of Dutch-led military forces. A glance at the manner of that defeat, however, also reveals much about the nature of Dutch power in the region during more normal times. The fatal weakness on the Minahasan side, as a descendant

---

56 Detailed accounts of the Tondano War based on Dutch archive sources have been provided by Eddy Mambu (1986) and Bert Supit (1986, 1991).

Mock duel in pacified Minahasa, 1839. Source: Meyer and Richter 1903, Tafel III.

of the Tondanese rebels bitterly recorded 60 years later, was less military than political.

> 'Tondano was to make the first move, unfurling the banner of revolt. [...] But a painful disappointment awaited the Tondanese. Only half of the people of Tomohon, under a chief named Lonto, remained true to the pact which had been made, and even they were quickly brought to heel by the Dutch troops who marched from Manado via Tomohon to Tondano. All of the other tribes left the Tondanese in the lurch and flocked to the side of the Government.' (Mangindaän 1873: 368.)

Many warriors from other parts of Minahasa, in fact, fought enthusiastically against the Tondanese in the ensuing war, returning to their villages only 'after they had punished the countrymen whom they had promised help and loyalty in time of danger' (Mangindaän 1873: 369). Nor was there any lack of bravery in the well-fortified water village of Tondano itself, where a small group of defenders held out for many months through siege, fire and famine until the last of those who failed to flee were 'cruelly massacred' in a final assault; the bones of their ancestors, for good measure, were then dragged out of their stone sarcophagi and burned to ashes together with the whole village, 'trees and all', by other

Minahasans acting on Dutch orders (Capt. L. Weintre to Res. Ternate, 7.8.1809, in ANRI Manado 61). Courage, as this war so dramatically demonstrated and as the Indonesian nationalists of a century later would always be painfully aware, was nothing without solidarity.

Why the Minahasan revolt unravelled almost before it had begun is difficult to reconstruct in detail, but the main factors are clear enough.[57] Some of its supporters were quickly bought off with gifts of cloth or alcohol, and in a classic example of another type of collective action dilemma (Lichbach 1995: 114-16) the defection, once initiated, snowballed automatically as more and more people more and more logically concluded (in the frank words of one defector) 'that it was not going to end well' (Graafland 1867-69, I: 284). The fact that the Tondanese were known and disliked both as mercenary headhunters (Mangindaän 1873: 366) and as social upstarts (Henley 1996: 49, 55) must also have tempted others to settle old grudges against them with Dutch help. A final factor is hinted at in a contemporary report by a pro-Dutch chief who witnessed the oath ceremony himself in June 1808. Whatever part a desire for liberation played in their actions, what the rebel leaders actually swore at Tondano according to this account was that as long as Dutch policies with respect to trade, tax and recruitment remained unchanged, 'they, the *hukum*, intended to be the Company and resident themselves' (zij Hukums de Compagnie en Resident zelfs wilde weesen).[58] Whether all of the conspirators repeated these words, or only the three main instigators (Lonto of Tomohon and two Tondanese chiefs), is not clear. Also uncertain is the extent to which the other delegates represented popular opinion in their home villages.[59] Against a backdrop of 'eternal rivalry', however, the magnitude of the political ambitions expressed at Tondano can hardly have failed to cause apprehension among those who suspected that in a free Minahasa, some *hukum* (to paraphrase George Orwell) would be more like residents than others.

Readers familiar with the ethnographic literature on South Sulawesi may be reminded here of Hendrik Chabot's cynical explanation for the Dutch rise to power in that part of the island:

---

57 In my earlier book on regionalism and nationalism in Minahasa (Henley 1996) I interpreted the absence of pan-Minahasan solidarity at the time of the Tondano War in terms of the lack of either a pan-Minahasan ethnic identity or a corresponding ideal of unity, which I saw as later developments. Closer inspection of the contemporary sources, however, shows that in fact both were already present, albeit perhaps not yet strongly developed, in 1808-9; what was still missing at this stage was the ability to translate them into political action by overcoming local enmity and distrust.
58 Statement by *hukum* Maramis of Klabat di Atas, 25.6.1808 (ANRI Manado 64).
59 According to the abovementioned eyewitness account, several important walak were represented not by their paramount chiefs but by 'lesser *hukum*'.

'The whole Bugis-Makasar country, every kingdom, every community, every village, every kinship group, and indeed every family containing more than one man, is potentially an arena of conflict. Within each of these groups, individuals struggle for more power [...] and are frustrated in this struggle by competition from their peers. For if a person believes that in a given situation he can best further his interests by not honouring a particular agreement, then he will betray it. Loyalty between equals with respect to mutual promises can never be counted on. [...] The VOC, and later the Netherlands Indies government, was seen [...] as a new power centre which they involved in their mutual oppositions and made use of in order to achieve their political goals. [...] If the VOC was attacked, it always received support from those who did not wish to see the attacker grow in strength.' (Chabot 1950: 122-3, 128-9.)

In this light it is tempting to interpret the considerable emphasis given to oaths of allegiance in both Bugis-Makasar and Minahasan cultures as the reflection of a counterfactual ideal. If adherence to such promises had been common, arguably, it would not have been necessary to seal them with desperate curses condemning traitors to be 'swept away like rubbish' (L.Y. Andaya 1978: 279) and 'pierced, pounded, hacked and crushed' (Riedel 1864b: 371) by agents of divine justice.[60] What weakened the power of these supernatural sanctions in practice, unfortunately, was that according to the prevailing *ex post facto*, 'might is right' conceptions of how divine justice worked, the end, if gratifying from an individual's point of view, quite literally justified the means (Aragon 1992: 245-51, 276-89; 2000: 186-201). Any failure of the invoked punishments to materialise following an episode of treachery, then, was likely to be interpreted as proof that the traitor enjoyed divine favour – something to which brave men always aspired.[61]

---

60 James Scott (1998a: 51) makes the same argument with respect to the emphasis on political loyalty in Malay historical texts, which he interprets as reflecting the actual prevalence of treason. The principle of counterfactuality of ideals - that people seldom idealise what they already enjoy - is probably one which deserves wider application in the field of Indonesian history.
61 Admiration for succesful treachery was particularly well developed in Minahasa, where the ancestral thief-hero Tumileng was believed to have introduced the most highly valued food staple, rice, after stealing this grain from the gods themselves in a daring feat of deceit (Schefold 1995). Also: Schouten 1998: 155, 263.

 # The stranger-king and his alternatives

In (after?) the era of nationalism, we are accustomed to regard shared ethnic identity as a factor conducive to effective cooperation, and ethnic differences as potential sources of conflict. In the past, however, the reverse was often true. In Minahasa, as the Minahasan anthropologist Paul Renwarin (2000: 55) has recently pointed out, most armed conflict seems to have taken place not across the language boundaries which formed the most important local ethnic divides, but between neighbouring villages or village federations within a single language community.[62] Relations between different language groups, by comparison, were more stable, reinforced in some cases by cultural stereotypes and joint rituals which portrayed them in terms of sexual complementarity (Henley 1996: 47). Historically speaking the most peaceful relationships of all, meanwhile, were those between the autocthonous groups and the most thoroughly alien component of the Minahasan political system, the Dutch government.

In order to understand this (for us) counterintuitive pattern, it is necessary to appreciate the limitations of the two principal endogenous sources of solidarity in these societies, kinship and gift-exchange. Marriage alliances, often skirting the borders of classificatory incest in order to limit the dispersal of land and other hereditable property down the generations (Renwarin 2000: 183; Schrauwers 1997: 367), were usually sufficient to hold together the descent groups constituting a single village or group of villages, but seldom provided a strong basis for

---

62 During the Tondano War, accordingly, the first groups to betray Tomohon and Tondano by defecting to the Dutch side were their immediate neighbours in the Tombulu language area (Graafland 1867-69, I: 284).

political integration on any larger scale.[63] Adultery, elopement, or divorce, moreover, could easily poison them, turning amity to enmity. The exchange of gifts, including military support and labour services as well as food, clothing and trade goods, was potentially a more inclusive source of solidarity; the competitive character of gift-exchange between parties of equal or near-equal status, however, meant that it too was liable to become a source of conflict. Kiefer provides a striking account of the volatility of exchange-based political alliances in Sulu, where warfare of a traditional kind persisted much longer than it did on Sulawesi due to the comparative weakness of state authority in the southern Philippines.[64]

> 'Now there is a very interesting characteristic of mutual gift giving [...] which bears on the problem of violence in Tausug society: usually the level and intensity of reciprocity can be increased much more easily than it can be decreased. It is possible to do more for the friend than he did for you, thus increasing his obligations when he reciprocates, but it is very difficult to do less; to break the chain of gift giving is not to go back to the earliest stages of the relationship, but to catapult it into hostility itself. [...] One can become more *of a friend* or *more of an enemy*, but one cannot decrease the level of friendship or enmity in a similar steplike manner. Only a total reversal of the relationship is possible. As a result alliances are very unstable, and today's friend may become tomorrow's enemy.' (Kiefer 1972: 65.)

An outsider whose dealings with members of such a society were too tenuous to elicit their friendship, then, was also distinctly less likely than a neighbour to become their declared enemy, and in a context of permanent readiness for war, the political advantage of never being actively hated outweighed the disadvantage of seldom being particularly liked either. The unemotional predictability of relationships between strangers, in fact, often provided a better basis for long-term trust than did the volatile intimacy of neighbours. The outsider's advantage was further enhanced by the fact that as an uninvolved bystander, he was in a good position to provide impartial arbitration when conflicts between insiders became intractable or intolerably destructive. Social solidarity tends to be heavily dependent on the confidence that in the event of a serious conflict, some kind of justice will be done; but justice requires a degree of impartiality on the part of the judges, and in small-scale, kinship-based societies, impartial judges who were

---

63 Among the Pamona Toraja of the Poso area in Central Sulawesi, the ideal marriage partners were third cousins. In the Minahasan village studied by Renwarin (2000: 180), only about 10% of marriages involve partners from other villages even today. The strikingly high incidence of albinism in Minahasa was sometimes attributed by Dutch observers to inbreeding (Bouvy 1924: 377), and many contemporary Minahasans agree.
64 Also: B.L. Foster 1977: 9-16; W.H. Scott 1994: 71.

not foreigners were hard to find. The more foreign the judge, in fact, the more effective he was likely to be in providing the kind of conflict resolution which would allow insiders to live harmoniously with one another.

This is probably a key reason not only why early Dutch expansion in Indonesia was often so successful despite the economic burdens which it entailed, but also for the general prominence of 'stranger-kings' in the history of eastern Indonesia and the Pacific. The phenomenon of the stranger-king is more often discussed in terms of cultural assumptions regarding the divinity of the exotic, and the fact that VOC judgements were regarded as *Godsspraken* (p. 40 above) indicates that such religious connotations were indeed present. Part of the reason for this, however, may have been that the ability to dispense impartial justice was itself perceived as something approaching a divine virtue. 'Impartiality in the strict sense of the word', noted Adriani (1916: 114), 'is not something which the Toraja expects from his fellow human beings; if he could imagine such a quality, he would find it superhuman [*bovenmenselijk*]'. Foreign interlopers, like pagan gods, were seldom loved; as kings, however, they enjoyed the important advantage of freedom both from the kin-based obligations which made impartial conflict resolution so hard to achieve in the societies which they colonised, and from the local jealousies and hatreds which made it so desirable. The rise of the colonial state in northern Sulawesi, then, can be regarded in part as a deliberately accepted solution to problems of mutual cooperation which were perceived by indigenous actors as difficult to solve without the aid of a powerful and impartial external party.

Critics of Hobbes' absolutist solution to those problems, of course, have often argued that in the long run, undemocratic states promote enmity among their subjects and undermine the ability to achieve peaceful cooperation on a broader societal basis.[65] Schrauwers (1997: 371-76), in the same spirit, stresses that lowland kingdoms like Luwu' in Central Sulawesi deliberately sowed disunity among their vassals by using them to punish each other for acts of disobedience to the *raja*, and alleges that the Dutch too 'governed by a process of divide and rule', obliging indigenous leaders to use them as conflict mediators and thereby installing themselves as 'key players in succession disputes and wars'. But at most that was half the story. For every upland group which smarted under headhunting raids permitted by a displeased *raja*, there were others who relied on the same *raja* for protection against aggressive neighbours (A.C. Kruyt 1908:

---

65 Pagden (1988), for instance, argues that the 'amoral familism' described by Banfield (1958) and others in the south of Italy originated in the 17th century when the Spanish rulers of the kingdom of Naples deliberately eroded earlier habits of cooperation and trust by sowing division among the existing political elite, undermining the local legal system, and implanting cultural values of private honour in place of public virtue.

1331). The fact that very similar patterns of feuding and headhunting were found in cognate societies inhabiting areas free from external intervention, such as the remote Cordillera Central of Luzon in the Philippines (Barton 1949, 1969), indicates that the motors of conflict were mainly endogenous. As for the Dutch, as often as they were able to manipulate indigenous conflicts to their own advantage, they were themselves manipulated, usually by vain promises of plentiful gold deliveries, into dangerous and expensive interventions which ended in ignominious withdrawal for either military or economic reasons.[66] Their provision of conflict mediation was not a cunning long-term strategy to reinforce their own influence, but a practical short-term policy designed to keep down the level of violence among their allies, thereby protecting their commerce (Godée Molsbergen 1928: 125, 137; Watuseke and Henley 1994: 372) and also minimizing the risk that protagonists in local wars would invite intervention by foreign parties other than the Dutch themselves. Their adjudication 'service', moreover, was clearly popular.

Except very briefly when faced with open rebellion during the Tondano War, at no point did the Dutch pursue a strategy of 'divide and rule'. In Minahasa, as in many other parts of Indonesia (Reid 1998b: 29, 34), their ideal throughout the VOC period was actually to unify the country under a single indigenous leader. As one exasperated Company official put it in 1744:

> 'In that case it would only be necessary to reach an agreement with one chief whenever we had to deal with these people, or they had to perform some service for the Company. At present, the situation is such that even in the most insignificant matter we must be content to beg and implore until all twenty village [*walak*] chiefs, with the same number of different opinions, arrive at a single sentiment.' (Godée Molsbergen 1928: 114.)

What ultimately convinced the Dutch that they had no choice but to continue dealing directly with each *walak* themselves was the intensified domestic warfare which, as already noted, followed each attempt to create superordinate indigenous chiefs with judicial authority above the *walak* level. According to indigenous oral history as recorded in the 1860s, one reason why the Spanish had been forced out of Minahasa in favour of the Dutch two centuries earlier was that they had made the even greater mistake of combining political with sexual favouritism:

---

66 'Mutual manipulation', as Fox (1977: 93) concluded in his historical and anthropological study of another part of eastern Indonesia, the island of Roti, is the best way to characterise relations between the Dutch and the indigenous groups with which they interacted in this period.

'And in those days a woman of the line of Lingkambene [from the Tondano area] invited her man, the leader of the Spaniards, to elevate her [and his?] son Muntu-untu to a position of great power, making him King [*Kolano*] over Minahasa. The Spaniards accepted this proposal, whereupon a bloody war broke out with the Tombulu [of the Tomohon area], who absolutely refused to accept a son of Lingkambene [as their ruler]. [...] Later the principal chiefs of the Tombulu [...] heard that another nation of white men, themselves no friends of the Spanish, were living in Ternate. So these four chiefs [...] travelled there to seek the friendship and help of the Dutch against the aggression of Bolaang Mongondow and the Spanish, accepting the *kumpania* as their mother and father.' (Riedel 1862: 51, 54-5.)

The ensuing establishment of a VOC fort in Manado triggered an anti-Spanish uprising in which the Dutch themselves played no part, but which nevertheless induced their rivals to abandon Minahasa for good in 1657 (ARA VOC 1225: 393v-5r; Waworoentoe 1894: 95). When some resentful Tondanese attempted to defy the Company four years later, as we have seen, a small number of VOC troops with a great deal of local support quickly forced them to desist, ushering in almost 150 years of unchallenged Dutch hegemony in Minahasa. To be successful, as experience in this and the subsequent colonial period confirmed, stranger-kings had to maintain an equal aloofness from all of their subjects.[67]

At worst, on the evidence presented so far, European intervention disturbed (typically at the deliberate request of particular indigenous parties) an already conflict-ridden political system in which any long-term stability depended less on 'contractual mutualities' (Reid 1998b: 32) than on a tense balance of military power. At best, it transformed such a system into a much more peaceful one based on the acceptance of a common judicial authority. Once followed, nevertheless, it is quite possible that the colonial short-cut to peace and order, straightforward and stable as it was, impeded any endogenous development in the same direction. In so far as it broke the cycle of blood feuding and thereby reduced the ambient level of hatred, an imposed peace prepared the ground for more spontaneous cooperation between former enemies. But in so far as people also became habituated to the use of colonial adjudication in the less violent disputes which continued to arise between them, they may well have been prevented from finding other ways of living peacefully together which, under the right circumstances, would have been available in the absence of a foreign state. Colonialism, in other words, became a sort of societal addiction which satisfied short-

---

[67] Considerable Dutch-Minahasan intermarriage did also take place (Henley 1996: 67-74), but never with such direct consequences in terms of political behaviour.

term needs at the expense of future options. For if Dutch officials often liked to portray themselves as the only real answer to the problem of indigenous violence, there is ample evidence that they were wrong here. While most parts of the region did remain in a state of endemic warfare until such time as they were brought under colonial control, there were also several areas where pacification predated European intervention.

In the first half of the nineteenth century, most strikingly, the autonomous territory of Bolaang-Mongondow, immediately to the south of Dutch Minahasa, underwent a rapid process of internal pacification in which all headhunting ceased and new unfortified settlements were laid out on a network of well-maintained bridle paths.[68] In 1857 the Dutch resident of Manado A.J.F. Jansen, having subjected Minahasa for four years to a uniquely harsh regime of colonial rule in the name of political tranquillity and economic progress, visited the uncolonised Mongondow plateau and declared himself 'amazed at the prosperity and order prevailing in this country' (Dagboek reis naar de noord- en westkust van Celebes 1857, in ANRI Manado 167).[69] Between about 1870 and 1900 a similar but less complete development of the same type, some aspects of which will be described below, took place in Mori (eastern Central Sulawesi). While eighteenth- and nineteenth-century Dutch officials liked to take exclusive credit for the domestic peace in Gorontalo, thirdly, the evidence is that this dated not from 1729, when a permanent VOC garrison was established there, but from 1673, when after many decades of conflict the two largest local chiefdoms, Gorontalo proper and Limboto, concluded a formal treaty of alliance which involved the leaders of both in each other's internal affairs, including the administration of justice (Bastiaans 1938: 221-2).[70] In the uncolonised Banggai archipelago, finally and most uniquely, nineteenth- and early twentieth-century Dutch visitors found no evidence that a headhunting tradition had ever existed.[71]

Dutch expansion in northern Sulawesi, we have seen, was based more on military, organisational and judicial abilities than on economic exchange. The VOC, in its European context primarily a commercial body, manifested itself here pri-

---

68 De Clercq 1883: 121; Riedel 1864c: 278; Veenhuizen 1903: 74; Schwarz and De Lange 1876: 162-4, 178; Wilken and Schwarz 1867b: 293.
69 This late episode of non-colonial state-formation was terminated by the imposition of a Dutch administrative and military presence in 1901, resistance to which cost 16 local lives (KV 1903: 91).
70 This does not mean that relations between the *Lima lo Pohala'a* and its neighbours in the same period were equally peaceful; the high levels of cooperation prevailing within the federation, indeed, enabled it to organise effective slave raids against other areas (Riedel 1870b: 556-8; Tacco 1935: 79).
71 Bosscher and Matthijssen 1854: 97; A.C. Kruyt 1932b: 249. In Gorontalo, by contrast, such a tradition had originally been present (Bastiaans 1938: 228), and in Mori the *raja* continued to sponsor headhunts against disobedient vassals at the end of the 19th century (Adriani and Kruyt 1900: 187).

marily as a state, and I have argued elsewhere that the definitive pacification of Minahasa by the Netherlands Indies government actually took place during a period of commercial stagnation (Henley, in press). In the looseness of its relation to commerce, however, colonialism was an unusual agent of pacification. In autonomous Bolaang Mongondow, the disappearance of war coincided with an expansion of foreign trade based on the export of cocoa and coffee from the fertile plateau in the interior where most of the population was concentrated, and of gold from the east coast.[72] Internal pacification in Mori after 1870 was associated with a growing export trade in the forest product *damar*, a type of conifer resin used in the manufacture of paints and varnishes (Schrauwers 1997: 373). The export product associated with state formation in Gorontalo was again gold; according to local tradition, one of the earliest *raja* of Gorontalo was himself a goldsmith (Bastiaans 1939: 26). Banggai, finally, was something of a commercial backwater by the nineteenth century, but 300 years earlier it had controlled the export of iron, a precious trade product later devalued by competition from Chinese and European imports, from several localities in eastern Central Sulawesi where iron ore was smelted and worked on a large scale.[73]

The association between trade and pacification rested on a complex combination of processes. Traditional subsistence farming, firstly, featured much seasonal underemployment of male labour, and war, according to Kruyt (1938, II: 55), was one of the activities (others included hunting and gambling) which 'filled up in an exciting way the time in which the men's labour was not required in agriculture'. Where profitable commercial employment became an alternative, then, interest in headhunting probably declined to some degree for reasons of time allocation alone. It is also possible that a sheer increase in the availability of resources had the effect of dampening social tensions, perhaps partly by eroding the assumption that economic life was a 'zero-sum game' in which one person's gain was another's loss (Hirschman 1958: 18-19). An outburst of intensified competition for the new sources of wealth, however, is equally conceivable under these circumstances (G.M. Foster 1965: 309-10), and Junker (1999: 343) has even argued for the existence of 'a long-term link between the development of long-distance maritime trading systems in Southeast Asia and the rise of maritime raiding and militarism'.

Another attractive 'egalitarian' interpretation of the relation between commerce and pacification proceeds from the observation that in order to trade, as

---

72 Riedel 1864c: 275, 277, 280, 283. Although one source from the 1860s states that Mongondow coffee served only for domestic consumption (Wilken and Schwarz 1867b: 287), some was certainly being exported by 1880 (Matthes 1881).
73 A.C. Kruyt 1901; Reid 1988-93, I: 110. Banggai was already the site of an important trading state in the 14th century (Ptak 1992: 29).

Marcel Mauss (1969 [1925]: 80) straightforwardly put it in his famous *Essai sur le don*, 'man must first lay down his spear'. By common consent of the Toraja tribes, according to one account of the late nineteenth-century damar trade boom, the Sumara valley in eastern Central Sulawesi was declared 'neutral territory', and placed out of bounds for headhunters, when it became the main route via which this product was exported (A.C. Kruyt 1930: 505). But exchange, as we have seen, could easily become a source of tension and conflict in itself, and whereas Mauss (1969: 80) believed that people could succeed in 'substituting alliance, gift and commerce for war, isolation and stagnation' simply by 'opposing reason to emotion and setting up the will for peace', much recent work in anthropology as well as economics underscores the importance of political institutions in policing markets, guaranteeing trade contracts, and preventing inflammatory acts of fraud.[74] Most known episodes of trade-related pacification in northern Sulawesi, certainly, are open to interpretation in terms of hierarchy as well as alliance.

A powerful alternative explanation for the Sumara valley 'peace pact', for example, is that Sumara fell under the higher jurisdiction of the *raja* of nearby Mori, whose sovereignty over this strategic area was actually said to have originated when he intervened in a conflict which had broken out there between resin collectors belonging to two different upland tribes (A.C. Kruyt 1900b: 437).[75] Elsewhere in the region, *raja* justified levies which they imposed on foreign traders partly by using their political influence to help guarantee (unwritten) contracts with local trading partners—an important service given that almost all commerce was based on long-term credit. In nineteenth-century Bolaang Mongondow, the 'gifts' which the captains of visiting trading vessels presented to the highest royal representative in a harbour settlement were said to be given 'less as anchorage fees than with the purpose of securing his assistance later with the collection of outstanding debts' (De Clercq 1883: 118). In the port of Palu (western Central Sulawesi) at the beginning of the eighteenth century, a local chief offended by the disrespectful behaviour of some Malay traders remarked that they would regret their effrontery next time they needed him to help recover debts owed to them by subjects of his in consequence of advances paid on slaves, gold and other export products (ARA VOC 1775: 225-6).

---

74 Useful surveys of the relevant literature here are provided in the volumes edited by Acheson (1994) and Drobak and Nye (1997); the essays assembled by Barlow (1999) begin to explore the relevance of the 'new institutional economics' to the study of Southeast Asian economies.

75 Another example of such ambiguity concerns the bilateral 'peace pacts', guaranteed by powerful kin groups with interests in mutual trade, which developed between formerly hostile communities in mountain Luzon in the early 20th century. Whereas some sources explain these pacts as spontaneous responses to the commercial opportunities created by new roads and trails (Barton 1949: 167-208; Dozier 1966: 212-35), others show that American colonial officials often inspired and organised them (Jenista 1987: 116-21, 258-9; Keesing and Keesing 1934: 137).

Indigenous states, indigenous strangers

While some thinkers have continued to see exchange (trade) itself as the basis for social solidarity even in complex economies, and the state (on balance) as a destabilising influence (Ridley 1996), the ethnographic evidence, particularly from Africa (Bates 1983: 21-58), suggests that when trade promoted pacification in traditional societies, it usually did so at least partly by encouraging political centralisation. The most peaceful and commercial societies of precolonial northern Sulawesi, certainly, were also the most hierarchical, both in terms of political and economic inequality and in terms of the extent to which they restricted social mobility. The coercive power of the Banggai state in its heyday is suggested by the fact that when the Spaniard Andrés de Urdaneta (1837: 437) arrived there in 1532, he witnessed the sacrifice of 'more than 150 men and women' during the funeral ceremonies of a single deceased ruler. In nineteenth-century Gorontalo the members of an hereditary elite, in their capacity as royal officials, received taxes and corvée labour services from the free population, also controlling a special group of royal slaves which served the incumbent political leaders regardless of their identity.[76] Private slave-owners, moreover, had lost the right to exclusive control over their own slaves, one category of which was obliged to perform the same corvée duties as free commoners (Pengaturan pusaka Gorontalo 1828, in ANRI Manado 18); Reid (1983: 19) identifies the restriction of private slavery as a key index of political centralisation and state formation in Southeast Asian societies. Of the 63 regulations included in a written legal code drawn

---

[76] Reinwardt 1858: 510-11; Riedel 1870a: 66, 74-5; Von Rosenberg 1865: 25-6; Scherius 1847: 403.

up by the raja and nobles of Bolaang Mongondow in 1856, 19 dealt purely with class privileges or the class status of children born to parents of unequal rank, while many others prescribed unequal penalties for infringements of the same rule by persons belonging to different social classes.[77]

Stratification like this reflected the unequal distribution of trade wealth. Geographical circumstances, I noted above, made it more difficult for chiefs in northern Sulawesi to monopolise trade than it was for their counterparts in many other parts of Indonesia. With the help of certain natural harbours and strategic overland routes, nevertheless, some did succeed in this to a considerable extent when commercial opportunities arose. 'Domestic trade', reported two Dutch missionaries after a trip to Bolaang Mondondow in 1866, 'is mostly in the hands of the *raja* and the highest officials of state [*rijksgroten*]'; the *raja* himself was the 'chief merchant' (*opperkoopman*), and the other nobles too 'all traders, as a result of which the population is more or less obliged to buy at outrageous prices' (Wilken and Schwarz 1867b: 296, 375).[78] Peripatetic between separate courts on the coast and in the interior, these trader-aristocrats reportedly made the best of what natural 'choke points' of trade were available to them by deliberately neglecting to improve the rugged mountain footpaths they used, the poor state of which was in striking contrast to that of the neat bridle paths and bridges on the plateau (De Clercq 1883: 117-18). A related reason for their 'concern to make the interior inaccessible', observed resident Jansen in 1857, was to conceal its wealth and the large size of its population from foreign rivals like the Dutch, 'in which up to now they have been supremely successful' (Uittreksel dagboek reis noordkust Celebes 1857, in ANRI Manado 167).

By dispensing gifts of foreign goods which could not be repaid in kind, and by staging feasts of honour on an unmatchable scale, such men tipped the seesaw of competitive exchange permanently in their favour and put others permanently in their debt.[79] By the same means, they were also able to build up personal followings of warriors with whose help they defended their commercial privileges and terrorised would-be rivals or recalcitrant subordinates. Following 'numerous complaints' by other chiefs, in 1879 the incumbent *raja* of Bolaang Mongondow was arrested by the Dutch during a visit to Manado and sentenced

---

77 Menopo 1893. It is likely, of course, that this code represented an elite ideal which was at least partly counterfactual; other sources, however, confirm that social stratification was pronounced in Bolaang Mongondow in the second half of the 19th century (De Clercq 1883: 123; Veenhuizen 1903: 68; Wilken and Schwarz 1867b: 314).
78 Also: De Clercq 1883: 124; Riedel 1864c: 283.
79 Often the two strategies were combined. In precolonial Minahasa, a lavish feast sometimes included the distribution of gifts to the guests (Schouten 1998: 102). In Central Sulawesi, visits by uplanders to their coastal *raja* were occasions for feasting on the meat of royal buffalo as well as exchanging rice and other upland products for salt and imported textiles (A.C. Kruyt 1938, I: 177-8).

to permanent exile for maintaining a 'robber band' which had killed at least 27 of his own subjects (KV 1880: 18; Rijkje Mongondo 1880). In part, then, the wealth of the elite promoted pacification simply by enabling it to buy friends and crush enemies.

Two other important pacifying effects of economic inequality, however, relate to the role of the elite as arbitrators rather than enforcers of the peace. Wealth, firstly, was a direct advantage to an arbiter, not only because disputants could reasonably expect it to make him less susceptible to bribery, but also because in conflict mediation as in other endeavours, money talked.[80] Next to blood, what most easily made angry men less angry was cash—or rather the valuable trade and heirloom goods, most importantly imported textiles, which provided the closest approximation to standardised currencies. Weregild or 'man-price', as in the pre-Hispanic Philippines as described by W.H. Scott (1994: 139), 'was argued as hotly as bride-price', and it did not always seem to matter whether or not blood money was actually paid by the enemy himself. If an arbitrator, instead of receiving compensation for his services from the disputants, could placate them with gifts of his own, then his effectiveness, and consequently also his status, was greatly enhanced. Padtbrugge noted that Company conflict resolution in Minahasa was 'especially' successful 'when, in some confused and unfathomable disputes, one or two *rijksdaalders*' worth of cloth are presented to the plaintiffs at the Company's expense in lieu of a fine on the other party' (Godée Molsbergen 1928: 64). By the beginning of the nineteenth century, it was standard practice when open warfare had already erupted for the Dutch to offer each party 'a piece of white cloth' as a prelude to peace negotiations (Memorie C.C. Prediger 30.6.1809, in ANRI Manado 61). In Central Sulawesi, Indonesian *raja* also distributed textiles in their capacity as peacemakers—or, more expensively, provided slaves for the warring parties to hack to death in order to dissipate their anger against each other, and at the same time by way of human sacrifice to mark the conclusion of hostilities.[81]

The second way in which social hierarchy promoted non-violent pacification, paradoxically, was by helping to overcome the problems of jealousy and perceived injustice which perpetuated Warre under more egalitarian conditions. The path to nobility was a difficult and dangerous one: under normal circumstances,

---

80 If all kinds of economic exchange were permeated with the social meanings attendant on giftgiving, all kinds of social relations were equally shot through with economic calculation. Besides in the importance of brideprice, weregild, and sacrifice, this 'hypereconomic' quality of social life is well illustrated by the fact that it was considered possible to expedite a difficult birth by placing a 'nice piece of cloth' on the mother's abdomen and promising this to the unborn child as an incentive (bribe) to emerge quickly (A.C. Kruyt 1930: 576).

81 Adriani 1901a: 158; A.C. Kruyt 1930: 527; 1938, II: 219.

jealous rivals of an emerging elite would do everything possible to cut it back down to size and prevent it from consolidating its position.[82] But there was also a threshold effect here: once a distinct class boundary had successfully been established, the situation tended to stabilise as the social distance between the classes lifted the nobility both above divisive favouritism in its treatment of its inferiors, and beyond their jealousy.[83] Chabot (1950: 102) hinted at this phenomenon when he wrote that whereas the relationship between equal or near-equal groups in South Sulawesi was 'best characterised as opposition', that between lord and vassal was 'based on cooperation'.[84] For an explicit account of part of the dynamic at work here, however, it is worth taking a longer ethnographic detour. Evans-Pritchard (1976 [1937]: 46) noted that among the Azande, whose society was competitive but sharply stratified, commoners seldom accused nobles of witchcraft, 'not merely because it would be inadvisable to insult them but also because their social contact with these people is limited to situations in which their behaviour is determined by notions of status'.

> 'A man quarrels with and is jealous of his social equals. A noble is socially so separated from commoners that were a commoner to quarrel with him it would be treason. Commoners bear ill-will against commoners and princes hate princes. [...] It is among householders of roughly equal status who come into close daily relations with one another that there is the greatest opportunity for squabbles [...].' (Evans-Pritchard 1976: 46-7.)

Whenever such 'squabbles' arose, of course, a noble was conveniently on hand to sort them out with lofty impartiality, thereby justifying his existence and his privileges. The stability of the class system, in other words, rested on the fact that nobles and commoners had effectively become strangers to each other.

In northern Sulawesi, royal status was framed in an idiom of strangeness even in those state-like polities where the ruling class was not, or no longer, distinct from the rest of the population in ethnic terms. In Gorontalo and neighbouring areas, for instance, the group from which the kings were chosen was said to be descended partly from foreign immigrants (including characters from

---

82 In modern Minahasa this is referred to with characteristic dark humour as *mahtetewelan* (Tombulu) or *baku cungkel* (Manado Malay), 'knocking each other down from below [like fruit out of trees with poles]' (Renwarin 2000: 12).

83 Hence, perhaps, the persistence of social stratification and internal peace in Banggai long after its decline as a trading centre (p. 59 above).

84 Some vertical cooperation, particularly between masters and slaves (Reid 1983: 7), involved an element of intimacy; in so far as hierarchy served to resolve conflict, however, intimacy between high and low was a liability to both.

the Bugis epic poem *I La Galigo*), and partly from semi-human creatures which had emerged from eggs, clumps of rattan, or shafts of bamboo long after the original peopling of the country.[85] Conceived as relative newcomers, the king and nobles were in this sense junior to their autochthonous subjects: in ritual and ceremonial language they were sometimes referred to as 'children', while commoners (or at least, village heads and the leaders of commoner kin groups) fell into 'parental' or 'grandparental' categories.[86] In Banggai, where the royal genealogy began with Javanese strangers invited by the population to bring peace and order in a time of anarchy when 'one man threw himself up as king, only to be driven out by another', each new *raja* actually sat on the lap of one of his subordinate chiefs during his inauguration and received a stern 'parental' warning against abusing his powers (A.C. Kruyt 1931: 518-19, 613).[87]

Before opting for a Javanese stranger-king, according to Banggai mythology, the people had first tried crowning a cat; in Limboto, comparably, the position of *raja* had successively been occupied for short periods by a stone penis, a rattan basket, and the egg from which the first (semi-)human ruler eventually emerged (Riedel 1870a: 114). At one level, these stories reflect a certain passivity on the part of the ideal king (less often, perhaps, on that of an actual ruler) which pioneer structural anthropologist F.A.E. van Wouden (1941: 406), in a little-known article on myth and society in Buol, linked with the function of the monarch as 'a symbol of the unity of the polity [*landschap*]'. Another obvious interpretation would be that the ideal of the passive ruler reflected a general fear of despotism. Both the passivity and the absurdity of the king and his non-human substitutes here, however, can also be seen as stylised and idealised solutions, inspired by a conviction that some kind of central authority is indispensable for the maintenance of social order, to the problem of finding a head of state who does not himself provoke destructive jealousy and rivalry. The metaphor of the child-king is an especially ingenious device in this respect, for while the wishes of a child, according to general opinion in Sulawesi, should be indulged wherever possible, few adults would think of being jealous of one.[88]

---

85 Bastiaans 1939: 29-31; Dunnebier 1949: 221-6; Riedel 1870a: 104, 114, Zainal Abidin 1974: 165-7.
86 Bastiaans 1938: 237; 1939: 33-4, 40, 45, 64-5, 69; Nourse 1999: 63; Van Wouden 1941: 335-6, 377-8. It is possible that the stratification into parental and grandparental as well as child groups reflects the rise and fall of successive stranger-king dynasties, and tempting to speculate that by intermarrying with the autochthonous population, each wave of immigrants prepared the way for the next by destroying its own usefulness as an alien element.
87 Banggai traded with Java for centuries and is mentioned in the 14th-century Javanese poem *Nagarakrtagama* (Robson 1995: 34).
88 Possibly this also sheds light on the strange mixture of respect and derision with which VOC officials, according to Ricklefs (1974: 27-30), were regarded on Java.

Under the right circumstances outsider status, which also conferred some immunity from jealous enmity, could be acquired as well as inherited. Earlier I cited the *mokole* of Mori as examples of stranger-kings, but strictly speaking this was misleading. Like their counterparts in Gorontalo and Banggai they were locally born, spoke the local language, and lived in close geographical proximity to many of their subjects. In another sense, however, they were indeed strangers—or rather, they increasingly came to resemble strangers as a result of the wealth and power which, in the last decades of the nineteenth century, they were able to derive from their control of *damar* exports through the Sumara valley. By taxing the resin traders the political elite of Mori, led by a *mokole* called Marundu, obtained unprecedented quantities of textile wealth for display, exchange and distribution (Schrauwers 1997: 373). In the process it also acquired, or at least elaborated, a mythical genealogy in which divine and foreign elements were combined.[89]

> 'The more the ruler of Mori grew in power, the more miraculous the stories about his ancestry became. A heavenly being, born out of a piece of bamboo, married a princess of Luwu' who was also a granddaughter of [the prophet] Mohammed; this being, named Lamale, was said to be identical to the sun-god of Central Sulawesi, Lasaeo!' (A.C. Kruyt 1900b: 454.)

The adoption of Islamic dietary and burial practices further accentuated the exotic aura of the noble group and its distinctiveness from the pork-eating, pagan commoners (Adriani and Kruyt 1900: 187, 195-6). Intermarriage between the two groups became less frequent and in time class differences, as W.H. Scott (1994: 138) said of some of the Philippine chiefdoms described in seventeenth-century Spanish accounts, were almost 'as natural as color of skin'. The *mokole*, in other words, was now a sort of indigenous stranger, standing 'above the people and to a certain degree outside the people' (J. Kruyt 1924: 64).

> 'We can say that a *mokole* is essentially a different type of person from an ordinary inhabitant of Mori; he is a different creature. Hence [...] the *adat* [custom] of the *mokole* must be treated quite separately from that of the common people. The basis of this otherness [*anders zijn*] is that the *mokole* has his origins in another country, 'heaven' (*langi*). Peoples' conception of this country is extremely vague [...]' (J. Kruyt 1924: 43.)

---

89 Both Schrauwers and the Kruyts (cited below) probably exaggerate the novelty of state formation in Mori, which had already been expanding at the expense of its neighbours in the 1850s (Uhlenbeck 1861: 4-5). Their accounts of how that process accelerated after about 1870, nevertheless, are generally valid.

When Nicolaus Adriani and Albert Kruyt first visited Mori in 1899 they noted that its population did not appear to be warlike and that its villages, unusually in Central Sulawesi, were not protected by defensive walls or pallisades. The reason for this, they were told, was 'the strong government of Marundu', who 'immediately intervenes in every dispute and brings it to a peaceful conclusion' (Adriani and Kruyt 1900: 204; A.C. Kruyt 1900b: 459).[90] Once alienated from his own people by trade wealth and recast as a semi-divine stranger, it seems, an indigenous leader was at last ready to provide the same kind of conflict management which made 'real' stranger-kings like the Dutch or the Bugis so useful, and which represented an important step toward ending the condition of Warre.

---

90 Also: Adriani and Kruyt 1900: 191-2.

10 Civility, faith, and the wages of sin

To a considerable extent, then, the pacifying influence of commerce was predicated on its association with aristocratic hierarchy and/or stranger-kings. The suppression of Warre under democratic conditions, as Hobbes and De Tocqueville well knew and as recent events in several parts of the world have reminded us, is a much tougher proposition. Nowadays the state in Indonesia, while stronger in military terms than its colonial predecessor and in principle more capable of enforcing a just peace among its subjects, is also irrevocably less foreign, and in that sense perhaps less likely to engineer one among its citizens.[91] While prosperity and a complex, interdependent economy undoubtedly help in situations like these, institutional changes are also essential. One important step, arguably, is the establishment of a legal and executive apparatus which is insulated from society at large not by ethnicity, class, or wealth, but by bureaucratic and legal rules which protect it from the subversion of kinship (nepotism) and gift-exchange (bribery); the ultimate goal is a 'civil society' in which all citizens are more or less estranged from one another by ingrained habits of impersonal civility as well as by the state-backed rule of law. Or perhaps the civil society must precede the bureaucratic state, lest the latter use its rule-based solidarity to

---

91 The dramatic increase in the range and complexity of social interactions since colonial times, on the other hand, has possibly compensated for this to some extent: a self-governing society large enough in geographical and demographic terms to generate a degree of anonymity in political and judicial processes, it can be argued, automatically stands a better chance of resolving conflicts impartially than does one in which most people are more or less distant blood relatives. Indeed, this may well be as important as military factors in explaining why it was often the small-scale societies of Indonesia which were the most vulnerable to colonial expansion.

uncivil ends; either way the endeavour is fraught with so many vicious circles of uncivility that as the Southeast Asia journalist Dennis Bloodworth (1975: 161) once observed, it 'calls for a stupendous act of faith' from millions of people who 'start by regarding a hovercraft society held up by nothing but an air-cushion of civic responsibility and loyalty to the constitution as no more feasible than a flying carpet'. In the recent calls for UN intervention in the troubled Moluccas, we can sometimes even hear an anachronistic attempt to bring back the stranger-king and his short-cut solution to the problem of Warre.

In its rule-boundedness, its egalitarianism and its incipient impersonality, returning to Sulawesi, the *mapalus* labour-exchange organisation as described in nineteenth-century sources can arguably be seen as a step, possibly inspired partly by Dutch bureaucratic models, in the direction of an internally rather than externally enforced system of social justice and collective action. In *mapalus* as in most other forms of *gotong royong*, however, the emphasis on working together in each other's physical presence was not just a matter of efficiency and sociability, but also had to do with keeping an essentially distrustful eye on each other and ensuring at first hand that everyone did their share. The use of corporal punishment, moreover, suggests that the inclination to break the rules was strong.[92] As an institution, *mapalus* promoted cooperation beyond the bounds of kinship and dyadic gift-exchange not by maximizing trust, but by minimizing the need for it. In more complex and sustained cooperative activities such intense mutual surveillance is often impossible, and greater ethical internalisation of impersonal rules of conduct is called for. Some authors have gone so far as to imply that what is neeeded here is a literal 'act of faith' in the form of conversion to a religion featuring a universalistic ethical system. Reid (1988-93, II: 151) proposes that Islam provided crucial social cohesion in the big cities of Southeast Asia during its first 'age of commerce' between 1450 and 1680, and Dobbin (1983: 125-6) has argued that the link between commercialisation and Islamisation in West Sumatra during the early nineteenth century must be explained partly by the way in which Islam provided an impersonal moral and legal code for market exchange.[93] More recently, according to Hefner (2000), the ethical and organisational resources of Islam have made it one of the most powerful forces for the development of a pan-Indonesian civil society.

---

92 *Mapalus* rules included specific injunctions against such tricks as 'turning over at the wrong time the hourglass used to determine the duration of the work', and 'covering up unturned ground with earth in such a way as to give the impression that it has already been worked' (*Mapalus en tuchtrecht* 1926: 268).
93 So closely was the Padri (militant Islamic) movement in early 19th-century Minangkabau associated with the reduction of 'transaction costs' (broadly: those reflecting distrust between the partners in an exchange) that in the markets which it controlled, goods changed hands without any bargaining (Dobbin 1983: 136).

This, of course, is risky theoretical ground where the polar temptations of cultural determinism and a functionalist interpretation of religion are equally strong. No doubt there are as many cultural routes to civil society as there are to capitalism; the evidence from Sulawesi, in any case, suggests that institutional change was usually prior to ethical change rather than vice versa. The Christianisation of Minahasa, for instance, had to wait for state-led pacification, prior to which any ethical injunction against killing as such could only be dismissed as dangerous nonsense.[94] To some extent, nevertheless, the relationship between institutional and ethical change must be a dialectical one, and the history of northern Sulawesi does support the idea of a link between religious conversion and indigenous state formation as well as indigenous trade. The partial Islamisation of the Mori elite during its period of commercial and political ascendancy in the late nineteenth century has already been described, and in Bolaang Mongondow more than half of the population became in some sense Muslim under the influence of its increasingly powerful trader-kings between 1830 and 1870.[95] There is even a possible Christian parallel: the Sangir islands enjoyed an unusually large degree of internal peace from as early as 1680 onward, and while regular Dutch conflict mediation was certainly an important factor here, it is also interesting to note that most of the Sangirese social elite was lastingly, if perhaps superficially, converted to Christianity by Spanish and Dutch missionaries in the course of the seventeenth century.[96]

While an extensive consideration of the relationship between religion and pacification would be too ambitious here, I would like to conclude this section with some speculation regarding the effect of religious change on the feasibility of political solidarity among equals—always the most precarious type. In emphasizing the importance of hierarchy as a solution to the problem of Warre, I have so far rather glossed over the fact that even the most centralised indigenous polities were typically dominated by an oligarchy of nobles among whom the paramount *raja*, chosen by his peers from a number of genealogically eligible candidates, was little more than *primus inter pares* (Von Rosenberg 1865: 18). The social structure, however hierarchical, was ultimately flat-topped rather than

---

94 The same goes, of course, for nationalism, another ideology which, however hateful some of its manifestations in practice, always presupposes that political behaviour should be based in the first place on amity rather than enmity.

95 The Islamisation of the Bolaang elite began in 1832 with the marriage of an Arab trader from Singapore to a daughter of the *raja* (Wilken and Schwarz 1867a: 277). By 1857 about half of the population of Mongondow was reportedly Muslim (Riedel 1864c: 277), and by 1866, two thirds (De Clercq 1883: 121).

96 Coolsma 1893: 193-210; C. Wessels 1935: 100-134. It is possible that these conversions were also associated with an expansion of the trade in coconut oil, which Sangir exported to Ternate and Manado.

pyramidal and if the unity of the state, however loose, was to be preserved, then members of the upper social stratum, at least, had to display a certain amount of spontaneous solidarity. In Gorontalo, moreover, the initial establishment of domestic peace seems to have been brought about not by the imposition of a new central power, but by a contractual fusion of the two most important existing polities, Gorontalo proper and Limboto (p. 58 above). Important provisions of the treaty which formalised this alliance in 1673 included guarantees that in the future each kingdom, rather than taking advantage of any internal dissent or rebellion faced by the other, would assist in suppressing it if necessary (Bastiaans 1938: 225).[97]

One source of such elite solidarity, as in the case of the Dutch and other foreign minorities, was no doubt shared contempt for non-members, combined perhaps with a disciplining fear of being excluded from the privileged group. Another was kinship: the marriage alliances of noble families were more wide-ranging than those of the lower classes, and wherever a sharp social stratification developed, the elites of rival chiefdoms tended to intermarry. Not the least reason for this was that high-status women, if they were to marry at all, often had no choice but to marry their enemies in order to avoid the direr prospect of marrying their inferiors.[98] Here again, however, we must note the fragility of marriage-based political alliances: according to local tradition, the wars between Gorontalo and Limboto began when a female ruler of Limboto, whose husband was raja in Gorontalo, committed adultery (Bastiaans 1938: 228). A third centripetal factor was economic complementarity: Gorontalo controlled the narrow trench linking the landlocked Limboto depression with the sea, a 'potential state space' of some importance by Sulawesi standards, but was rather short of arable land for food production, of which Limboto had an abundance. Sexual complementarity being the strongest indigenous cultural model for cooperation between equals, the resulting upstream/downstream exchange relationship (Bronson 1977) found expression in myth and ritual as a sexual opposition between 'male' Gorontalo and 'female' Limboto (Korn 1939: 77-84). The exchange in question, however, did not involve the most important export product, gold (which was produced by both polities from mines in satellite settlements outside the Limboto depression), and neither economic nor symbolic complementarity prevented the two kingdoms from invoking the assistance of foreign powers

---

97 The 19th-century legal code of Bolaang Mongondow (pp. 61-2 above), comparably, included the provision that runaway slaves were to be returned to their original master rather than offered protection by his rivals (Menopo 1893: 491).

98 It follows that intermarriage among the elites of rival polities such as Ternate and Tidore in the North Moluccas cannot necessarily be regarded, as Leonard Andaya (1993: 55) claims, as good evidence for a deep underlying amity between them.

(Ternate and Makassar) in a series of disastrous wars which they fought against each other in the sixteenth and early seventeenth centuries.[99]

A final and more unique factor favouring elite solidarity in the case of Gorontalo and Limboto, arguably, was that these were the first parts of northern Sulawesi where Islam, apparently introduced from Ternate in the late sixteenth century (Bastiaans 1938: 231-2), began to make converts on a substantial scale. The 1673 treaty appears to have been conceived and sponsored by the chief Islamic religious official in Gorontalo, *khatib* (later *raja*) Eato, a man also remembered in oral tradition for promoting the replacement of customary law by the *shari'a* (Nur 1979: 221). The text of his treaty, which has fortunately survived, is framed partly in an Islamic idiom, ending with quotations (in Arabic) from the Koran, with a declaration that 'as God forsakes not his promises, neither shall the *negeri* Gorontalo and Limboto change their agreement', and with the oath 'by God, by the word of God, by the prophet of God' (Bastiaans 1938: 224, 247).

Pagans, as we have seen, also had frequent recourse (partly for want of more mundane alternatives) to supernatural justice for the purpose of contract enforcement as well as conflict adjudication, swearing graphic oaths in which they called various kinds of sickness and suffering on themselves in the event of a breach (p. 52 above). A fundamental problem with this deterrent, however, was that as in the case of the Tondano War, the familiar gods often demonstrably failed to punish perjury or treachery, thereby strengthening the general belief that they were scarcely less fickle, manipulable or partisan than mortals.[100] Conversion to Islam or Christianity, it has often been observed, put a much greater distance between man and the sacred (Reid 1988-93, II: 159). God, in other words, became more of a stranger, and by the same token a fairer and sterner judge whose sentences, as Kruyt proudly observed of his Christian converts in Central Sulawesi, were less lightly ignored.

> 'The heathens also expect punishment in certain cases [of sin], but if this does not materialise, then either the [magical] countermeasures employed have been strong enough, or the gods have been particularly lenient. Among the Christians the feeling has arisen that the punishment for such a transgression is inevitable, and that if the sinner does not experience it in this life, then he will receive his just deserts in eternity.' (A.C. Kruyt 1926: 114.)

---

99 Bastiaans 1938: 227-36; Riedel 1870a: 106-8, 115-16; Tiele and Heeres 1886-95, III: 358-9, 388-90.
100 According to some (possibly exaggerated) local accounts as recorded by J. Kruyt in the early 20th century, the use of traditional legal oaths in Mori had long ago fallen into disuse 'when people came more and more to the realisation that the calamities which had been invoked did not take place even when the testimony was false' (J. Kruyt 1924: 98).

Despite the importance of the ancestral dead in traditional religion, pagans in Sulawesi had always been sceptical of any specific claims regarding the nature of life after death. 'They had no belief in resurrection, judgement, or hell', complained a Jesuit missionary on Siau in the 1580s, 'and if I spoke to them of these things they were derisive, saying: Who has seen that? Who has come back from there?' (H. Jacobs 1974-84, II: 266-7).[101] Padtbrugge, after a conversation with a Minahasan ritual expert in 1679, had an even stronger impression of religious and ethical this-worldliness.

> '[N]either do they believe in the immortality of the soul, holding instead that this decays with the body, so that good and evil are not judged and punished or rewarded in the hereafter, but rather in this life, while a person still exists. [...] Thus honour and prosperity in this world are the only rewards of virtue, and [...] among the punishments for sin they reckon all bodily sufferings, diseases, and plagues, so that for them this world is itself a heaven or a hell [...] according to how well or badly one lives [...]' (Padtbrugge 1866: 312.)

The postponement of hell into the hereafter, of course, made divine justice doubly frightening by putting its inevitability safely beyond falsification. The 1673 Gorontalo-Limboto treaty, strikingly, condemned those guilty of infringing its otherwise largely unenforceable rules not only to misfortune in this life, but also to punishment 'in the fires of hell, from which we seek God's protection' (Bastiaans 1938: 224).[102]

Game theorists call the fear of delayed punishment for current opportunism 'the shadow of the future', and have shown in great detail how crucial it is to the possibility of rational cooperation in situations where betrayal is tempting (Axelrod 1990: 126-32). Conversion to Islam or Christianity, at least in theory, darkened that shadow by extending the relevant future beyond death. For early modern Europeans, it is worth remembering, the link between divine justice and social solidarity was self-evident: even John Locke, in his famous *Letter concerning toleration* of 1689, warned that 'those are not at all to be tolerated who deny the being of a God', since '[p]romises, covenants, and oaths, which are the bonds of human society, can have no hold upon an atheist' (Locke 1961 [1689]: 93).

---

101 Very similar complaints occur in much later missionary and colonial literature (Riedel 1872: 490; Woensdregt 1930: 609-10).
102 The Bugis/Makassar treaty curses discussed by Andaya (1978: 279-80), by contrast, mainly seem to have been pagan and this-worldly in content.

11 Patterns and parallels

Failing either a sufficiently credible divine justice or a sufficently effective civil justice, royal or foreign justice often remained an attractive alternative, and this attraction fuelled the expansion of both indigenous and colonial states in Indonesia and elsewhere. Perhaps the best-known examples of European stranger-kings in Southeast Asian history are the 'white rajahs' of the Brooke dynasty who ruled Sarawak between 1841 and 1941. Studies of the Brooke regime emphasise that its success in displacing indigenous conflicts from the military to the judicial sphere, in the form of highly popular government law courts, was an essential element in the pacification of Sarawak alongside the selective exploitation of local enmities for military purposes (Pringle 1970: 170-73, 190-93; Wagner 1972: 155-6, 177). Jenista (1987: 242-51) sees this as part of a more general pattern in late-colonial Southeast Asia whereby formerly stateless hill peoples, including the Kachin and Shan of Burma and the Ifugao of Luzon as well as the Iban of Sarawak, developed close political relationships with the European coloniser; among the several factors involved here, Jenista concludes, was a widespread appreciation for the benefits of colonial pacification and conflict resolution.

A more surprising parallel comes from seventeenth-century Dutch Taiwan, where the VOC, facing an array of warlike tribal communities similar to the Minahasan *walak*, managed to acquire a political supremacy even more impressive than it enjoyed in Minahasa at the same period. Here internal warfare, as well as resistance to the Dutch, ended almost completely following the defeat of one of the most powerful aboriginal groups, Matou, by a coalition of 500 Company soldiers and their local allies in 1635.

> 'Indeed, the aborigines of Taiwan appear generally to have been willing subjects. Many submitted of their own accord, and often readily, to Dutch rule. To be sure, many were motivated to join out of fear of their fellows. Since the towns were continually at war with one another, the Company's presence brought about a great shift in the balance of forces on Taiwan: towns allied with the Company were assured protection from their traditional enemies [...]' (Andrade 1997: 81.)

While this author emphasises the military (and ideological) aspects of Company rule in Taiwan, it is sufficiently clear even from the admittedly partisan VOC sources that fear and the changed balance of military power were not the only factors here.[103] Another was the public adjudication of local disputes by Company representatives, which was as popular in Taiwan as in Minahasa, and which took place from 1641 onwards at an annual *landdag* or 'day of state' when the leaders of all the aboriginal communities gathered to take part in ceremonies and feasting under VOC auspices (Andrade 1997: 71-2). The Dutch peace, whether legislated or imposed, was also widely appreciated for its own sake:

> 'It was delightful to see the friendliness of these people when they met for the first time, to notice how they kissed one another and gazed at one another. Such a thing had never before been witnessed in this country, as one tribe was nearly always waging war against another [...] and if we had not influenced them, they would never have been mutually united; for formerly no one dared to address the other, no one trusted the other, and to practice deception as much as possible was the general rule.' (Campbell 1903: 130-31.)

Some sources on later episodes of European expansion in Southeast Asia are more explicit that the benefits of peace, the most basic of all public goods, were already anticipated by its recipients prior to the pacification itself. According to one recent ethnohistorical study based on indigenous sources, for example, the Dutch invasion of Kerinci (upland Jambi, Sumatra) in 1903 was actively supported by a large section of the local population which welcomed the colonial government as a 'stabilising force', and 'hoped the Dutch would bring an end to in-

---

103 One immediate difficulty with the 'shift in the balance of forces' interpretation is that the peak troop strength of the VOC in Taiwan was not only much smaller than that of all its vassal groups combined, but apparently also smaller than that of some of them individually. Matou alone could field a force larger than that of 500 Europeans which led the attack on it in 1635, and at least one other nearby 'village' was bigger still (Blussé, Van Opstall and Ts'ao Yung-Ho 1986: 377; Campbell 1903: 179-80). In Minahasa, some of the indigenous *walak* boasted fully ten times more fighting men (Van Dam 1931: 74-5) than the force of 65 VOC soldiers which, with much local help, 'disciplined' rebellious Tondano in 1661 (p. 24 above).

ter-village disputes and introduce law and order into the area which was renowned for its lawlessness' (Watson 1992: 35).

The attraction of conflict resolution by powerful and impartial outsiders is confirmed by the mythologies, as well as the morphologies, of many indigenous Southeast Asian kingdoms. Especially striking here is the Hobbesian idiom in which the Bugis and Makasar peoples of South Sulawesi explained the origins of their kings, whom they credited with divine descent, in a past era when their homeland had been divided (like the north of Sulawesi at later times) into small and mutually hostile tribal communities.[104]

> 'There were many of these *gaukeng* community complexes throughout South Sulawesi, and before long they began to impinge upon each other and disputes began arising, especially over land and water rights. Force was often used to solve a dispute because there was no other mediating mechanism available to settle inter-*gaukeng* community quarrels. [...] This period is characterised in tradition by an especially graphic description of man being like fish, with the larger and stronger consuming the smaller and weaker. In desperation the people appeal to the gods to send a ruler to earth [...] so peace and order can be restored.' (L.Y. Andaya 1981: 12.)

In Sumatra, too, oral traditions regarding the origin and function of kingship emphasised the need for external intervention in those local conflicts which could not be resolved by means of negotiation and compromise at the local level.

> 'On occasion, however, it was impossible to reach a compromise, and in these cases it was necessary to have recourse to a higher authority. A familiar theme in legends throughout the area is thus the appeal to some distant ruler at a time of anarchy and discord, for the purpose of kings was to provide wise counsel when necessary and dispense judgments all would observe.' (B.W. Andaya 1993: 31.)

The role of the (otherwise rather mysterious) Minangkabau *raja* as arbiters of disputes and providers of justice (*keadilan*) is particularly well documented in both indigenous and European sources.[105] Here again there was a strong supernatural association: the justice of the Minangkabau ruler 'emanated from God' (Drakard 1999: 230) and reflected the role of the king as God's representative on earth.

---

104 Also: Bulbeck and Caldwell 2000: 8; Pelras 1996: 32, 110.
105 Dobbin 1975: 78; Drakard 1999: 229-30; De Josselin de Jong 1951: 103, 107.

The link between the divine or oracular character of stranger-kings and their judicial function is very much evident in the literature on Africa, where anthropologists have tended to display a stronger awareness of the Hobbesian problem of order and disorder than have most of their counterparts in Southeast Asia.[106] Stranger-kings of various descriptions were a widespread feature of precolonial African societies; throughout a large part of East Africa, for instance, indigenous political systems were characterised by 'the domination of chiefless societies by immigrant aristocracies' (Southall 1970: 229). In many cases, such as that of the Alur in Uganda, these dominant foreign groups were seen less as invading conquerors than as invited guests:

> 'The peoples who became subject to Alur chiefs recognized the right of retaliation for wrongs and, as they now remember their own past, did not have any formal means of bringing hostilities to an end. They were not conquered in battle by the Alur. They acquiesced in the extension of Alur rule, and some of them even asked an Alur chief to give them one of his sons as their ruler; and one of their principal reasons for wanting a ruler was so that he could settle their quarrels.' (Mair 1962: 58.)

The Alur chieftain was a ritual expert and rainmaker as much as a warrior, and in the eyes of his foreign subjects his ritual power 'sanctioned his authority as an arbitrator' (Southall 1970: 246). Among the Ibo of southeastern Nigeria up to about 1920, a similar role was played by an allochthonous elite minority known as the Aro (Northrup 1978: 114-45; Ottenberg 1958). The authority of the Aro, who called themselves 'children of God', rested partly on their role as 'agents' of the supernatural oracle Aro Chuku, to the judgement of which the stateless Ibo often deferred when local wars and other conflicts could not be resolved by other means. It was also reinforced, however, by Aro control over vital trade routes and groups of mercenary warriors.

> 'The Aro [...] organized trade in southeastern Nigeria and provided as well a system of internal justice and military protection. [...] The Aro were themselves traders; they provided protection for trade; and they provided the 'Oracle'—a judicial system for resolving disputes without taking recourse to

---

106 One reason for the contrast is that colonial pacification was often a later event in Africa than in Southeast Asia; another may be the well-known 'Orientalist' tendency of Southeast Asianists to emphasise the exotic and aesthetic aspects of indigenous cultures. The work of R.F. Barton (1938, 1949, 1969) on the tribal Philippines, similar in focus to that of politically-orientated Africanists like Evans-Pritchard (1940) and Gluckman (1965), forms an important exception here.

feuds. These advantages led to their rapid expansion [...] as local communities called them in.' (Bates 1983: 24.)

If for 'Aro' we substitute 'Dutch', then it seems to me that this summary is almost equally applicable to many parts of Sulawesi up to the beginning of the twentieth century. In the African context itself, perhaps not surprisingly given the late date and military character of much European expansion in that continent, parallels between traditional and colonial stranger-kings are seldom drawn.[107] That they sometimes existed, nevertheless, is suggested by the case of the early nineteenth-century British Gold Coast administrator George Maclean, a man whose career was compared by his biographer Metcalfe (1962: viii) to that of his contemporary James Brooke in Sarawak.[108] In the period of trading company rule up to 1822, it had already been common on the Gold Coast that 'disputes between Africans, in which no European was involved, were brought to the castle for the Governor's mediation' (Metcalfe 1962: 170). Under Maclean's direction this practice was developed into a systematic judicial institution, backed up on occasion by punitive military expeditions, which both cemented the position of the British in the area and helped to weld its diverse peoples into a single political unit. In the testimony of Frank Swanzy, an out-station commander under Maclean from 1834 to 1842:

> '"I was called upon to interfere [by] settling and arbitrating in palavers of all kinds, and of almost every nature, which they brought to the fort in preference to settling among themselves." [...] On average, Swanzy estimated that he spent two hours a day hearing palavers. The penalties imposed were often too light for the liking of the injured party, but he never had any difficulty in getting his decisions accepted. On one point he was emphatic. The growth of this jurisdiction was the Africans' own doing; "they have forced it upon us".' (Metcalfe 1962: 178.)

Maclean himself, who cultivated an aloof and mysterious image, acquired an honorific title meaning 'peacemaker' and reportedly became the object of religious veneration.

---

107 Southall (1970: 230-34) explicitly denies the validity of any such parallel in the Alur case, arguing that (late-)colonial rule in Africa was based much more heavily on military superiority. With respect to the desire for military protection, on the other hand, the role of indigenous agency in colonial expansion is well established in the African literature, some of which characterises the partition of the continent as resulting less from a European 'scramble for Africa' than from an African 'scramble for protection' (Caplan 1969) against African enemies - albeit often enemies rendered more dangerous than before by the backing of their own European protectors.
108 I am grateful to Martin Klein for drawing my attention to this source.

A final example of institutionalised adjudication by strangers which is worth mentioning here comes not from Africa or Asia but from medieval Europe, and is described by Avner Greif in his contribution to the influential institutionalist political science anthology *Analytic narratives* (1998). In the thirteenth and fourteenth centuries the city of Genoa, like several other Italian city-states, routinely hired a non-local leader called a *podestà* on a fixed-term (typically one-year) contract to serve as its supreme judge and administrator. Each new foreign *podestà* brought with him an independent military force strong enough to keep the peace between any two of the clans which dominated and periodically threatened to destabilise domestic political life, but not strong enough to impose his will on the Genoese in the face of concerted opposition. In order to preserve his impartiality, he and his relatives were 'restricted from socializing with Genoese, buying property, getting married, or managing any commercial transactions for himself or others' (Greif 1998: 53) – he was emphatically to remain, in other words, a stranger.[109]

Stranger-kings varied greatly in the strength of their control over the means of violence. At one extreme were arbitrators or mediators who had little independent means of enforcing their decisions, and whose authority derived mostly from their perceived impartiality and/or supernatural qualities: examples arguably include the Minangkabau kings in Indonesia.[110] This was the least costly and dangerous form of centralised conflict resolution, but perhaps also the least reliable.[111] At the opposite end of the spectrum were situations in which the alien group had established a true state, in the sense of securing a near-monopoly on the use of violence and using this monopoly to enforce a permanent peace. The theatres of Dutch expansion discussed above all entered this stage at an earlier or a later date: Taiwan in the seventeenth century, Minahasa in the nineteenth, and Central Sulawesi in the twentieth. Intermediate between the two extremes (often in time as well as in form) lay diverse political compromises which, as in the case of medieval Genoa, involved elements of both arbitration

---

109 He was further required to move his residence periodically to a new quarter of the city in order to avoid associating for too long with any single clan; peripatetic behaviour, strikingly, was also widespread among the *raja* of northern Sulawesi in the 19th century (Bastiaans 1938: 227; Van der Hart 1853: 113; Henley 1996: 30; A.C. Kruyt 1931: 525; Sarasin and Sarasin 1905, I: 91; Steller 1866: 36-7).
110 Institutionalised conflict mediation by relatively powerless third parties, of course, is also common in many modern contexts (Wall and Lynn 1993).
111 One problem with this kind of system was that as far as pagans were concerned, the mark of truly divine justice tended to remain practical efficacy. Lasting faith in the divine status of a judge whose verdicts were not often seen to be enforced, then, may well have been limited to peoples which, like the Islamic Minangkabau, already believed in the inevitability of eschatological justice, and consequently had relatively less need of worldy enforcers anyway.

and enforcement. In Dutch Minahasa prior to the military pacification of 1809, and in the Bugis-dominated kingdoms of Central Sulawesi, private vengeance and feuding continued to be possible, the alien authorities intervening only at the active request of one or both parties in a given local conflict; to flout their judgement after they had become involved, nevertheless, was to invite military (judicial) punishment.

The stability which such compromises sometimes acquired reflects the fact that powerful forces militated against the acceptance of more complete state control. These included jealousy and resentment of the powerful, scepticism regarding their ability or will to enforce a just peace, and the well-founded expectation that if they obtained still more power, they would use it to increase their own wealth by imposing a heavier burden of tribute or taxation on their subjects.[112] What can be also discerned behind all of the stranger-king systems, nevertheless, is an equally realistic awareness of the functionality of political centralisation or hierarchy, especially a hierarchy surmounted by a foreign or otherwise exotic and socially isolated group, in helping to control the ever-present threat of disorder and conflict. The progression from 'alien diviner' (Colson 1966) to colonial Leviathan remains a continuum; even at its most critical phase, the permanent disarmament and pacification of the indigenous population, people were often willing to give up the tradition of 'taking the law into their own hands' on the critical condition that the (alien) state also forced all their (familiar) neighbours to do the same. Given sufficient confidence in a successful outcome that would preclude future revenge attacks—and/or, as in the case of the Tondano War, insufficient confidence in the outcome of attempts at resistance—many were even prepared to participate in the pacification process themselves by taking up arms, temporarily and for the last time, against any dissenting minority.

Hierarchy, of course, is not the only potential solution to the problem of Warre, and given time it is possible that the autonomous growth of economic exchange and interdependency, or the spread of the impersonal ethics associated with the world religions, would in themselves have been sufficient to overcome vicious circles of distrust, hostility and violence. The empirical evidence from northern Sulawesi, however, suggests that in practice both trade and religious conversion were themselves closely associated with, and to some extent predicated upon, state formation—a means of pacification which was in any case easier to promote in an instrumental way thanks to the ready availability of foreign groups well suited to play the role of stranger-king.

---

112 Pre-colonial states in Africa, notes Bates (1983: 41), were simultaneously both exploitative and benevolent: by generating public goods, such as the peace necessary for trade, ruling elites were also able to secure disproportionate economic benefits for themselves.

12 Concluding remarks

Inspecting the pacified or half-pacified remains of tribal societies, even the most knowledgeable and cynical scholars have sometimes been tempted to idealise life under stateless conditions. After eight years spent among the Ifugao of mountain Luzon at the beginning of the twentieth century, for example, the political anthropologist R.F. Barton (1969 [1919]: 3) declared himself 'convinced' that thanks to their 'well-developed system of laws', the Ifugao had 'got along very well in the days before a foreign government was established among them'. Yet his own reconstruction of the normal state of Ifugao society, which can fairly be described as one of perpetual feuding and fear, reads like a Hobbesian treatise on the inability of 'small Families', however strong their concern with law and justice, to translate that concern into peace and order without having recourse to a higher judicial and executive authority.[113]

> 'The Ifugao has no tribunals to sentence, and no government to execute. [...] Doubtless no two nations or tribes of the world ever engaged in a warfare in which each did not consider the other the aggressor, or at least, the offender. The same is true with respect to feuds between families, which were almost as numerous as the families themselves. [...] We must substitute, however, for

---

113 The Ifugao autobiographies which he later collected (Barton 1938) do nothing to resolve this contradiction. We might also question whether stateless peoples like the Ifugao really enjoyed 'true freedom' as Barton (1969: xxi) claimed, or whether there is not more truth in Ernest Gellner's memorable dictum (1995: 33) that 'traditional man can sometimes escape the tyranny of kings, but only at the cost of falling under the tyranny of cousins'; but that is another story.

patriotism, fraternal and filial love; the sense of duty to the unavenged dead, love of vengeance, and intense hatred engendered and justified by a well learned catalogue of wrongs and assassinations inflicted on the family by the enemy family. Once started, a blood feud was well nigh eternal (unless ended by a fusion of the families by means of marriage), for the reason that what was a righteous execution to one family was a murder (usually treacherous) to the other.' (Barton 1969: 68.)

Not surprisingly against this background of Warre, oral history indicated that in the late nineteenth century Spanish soldiers had been 'invited' into Ifugao as military allies by the people of one district, Kiangan (Barton 1969: 98-9). That neither political independence nor the freedom to kill were in themselves particularly dear to the Ifugao was confirmed a few years later during the US occupation, when despite the imposition of unpaid roadbuilding duties, two platoons of American-trained Ifugao policemen armed with single-shot Springfield rifles (Jenista 1987: 56), together with a series of large government-sponsored feasts, were sufficient to bring about the rapid pacification of a warlike population almost 100,000 strong. As in Sulawesi, another very important factor here was a new kind of impartial conflict resolution. In a later account by an Ifugao historian it is the main agent of colonial justice during the pacification period, the police officer J.D. Gallman, who appears in the by now familiar role of the peacemaking stranger-king.[114]

> 'Gallman befriended the "chiefs" of the villages and initiated peace pacts among them. In the peace pact ceremony (*hidit*) the feuding parties met with an arbiter and promised not to fight each other any more. [...] His dedication and impartiality in dispensing justice and, above all, his proven bravery and fighting prowess won the respect and admiration of the Ifugaos. The people confidently referred to him in all cases of dispute and his fast but just decisions won the support of everybody. When disagreement arose, the people would say, "*Na nga mong man hi Gallman*", meaning "It's up to Gallman". They knew that the *Malikano* (American) would give the right verdict. This phrase was so popular that even recently, people would still quote it.' (Dumia 1979: 35.)

---

[114] In the pacification of the neighbouring Kalinga people, the administrator W.F. Hale played the same role as Gallman among the Ifugao and acquired a similar reputation (Dozier 1966: 38-40; Jenista 1987: 70, 258-60).

CONCLUDING REMARKS

Batavia, 1929: loyalist Minahasans celebrate their historic 'alliance' with the Dutch by re-enacting the establishment of a VOC presence in Manado more than 250 years earlier. The standing figure represents VOC Governor of the Moluccas Simon Cos. Above: governor-general A.C.D. de Graeff looks on. Source: Pandji Poestaka *5:72 (15 January 1929).*

'The Americans' lack of kin in Ifugao', adds another ethnohistorical study, 'was frequently cited by informants as a reason for their good decisions' (Jenista 1987: 119).

The various tiny military actions fought in this period served not to terrorise the people as a collectivity (an impossible feat under the circumstances), but rather to reassure the people as individuals (and families) that if the need arose the state was capable of terrorizing their neighbours, thereby relieving them of personal responsibility for this dangerous task and justifying its own claim to a monopoly of violence. When the Americans finally imposed a total ban on the carrying of weapons in 1914, there was reportedly 'immediate compliance' and 'hearty cooperation' on the part of the Ifugao (Dumia 1979: 43). A similar dynamic, I would suggest, had probably been at work during the original 'conquest', centuries earlier, of millions of lowland Filipinos by the Spanish, whose entire occupation force 'initially numbered about 500 and probably never exceeded a few thousand during the early colonial period' (Newson 1998: 25).[115]

The fact that more than 300 years separated the pacification of lowland Luzon from that of the nearby mountains, on the other hand, is a reminder that despite all that has been said above about the real and perceived advantages of foreign rule to stateless peoples, colonial expansion was seldom an automatic or inevitable process. As in the case of the Dutch in Sulawesi, the Spanish expansion in the Philippines was characterised by long interludes of stasis and resistance. W.H. Scott (1974), in fact, has described the whole history of contact between the Spanish and the upland peoples of Luzon, from the sixteenth century to the end of the nineteenth, in terms of a largely effective indigenous struggle against foreign aggression in which each local alliance made by the Spaniards was immediately counterbalanced by enhanced resistance from the traditional enemies of those who had chosen the invader's side.[116] If the logic of the pacifying stranger-king as compelling as I have implied, and if it served the Americans so well among the Ifugao, why then did it fail the Spanish colonial state in the same area for so long? What factors, in other words, determine whether a given stateless group will welcome or reject the advance of a foreign

---

115 Conventional explanations, in so far as these can be said to exist, stress the allegedly greater superiority of Spanish arms under lowland conditions (W.H. Scott 1974: 6), the straightforward inability of the politically fragmented Filipino population to form a common front against the invaders (Phelan 1959: 9, 15), and the success of Catholic missionary efforts (Hall 1968: 248). Regarding the second possibility, it should be noted that the uplanders were no less divided than the lowlanders; regarding the third, that a considerable amount of unsuccessful missionary activity also took place in upland Luzon during the Spanish period, suggesting that here as in Sulawesi, European political dominance was a precondition for Christianisation rather than vice versa.

116 During the 19th century alone, 75 Spanish military expeditions took place in the Cordillera Central (W.H. Scott 1974: 7).

CONCLUDING REMARKS

power, and whether the outcome for a cluster of such groups will be collective submission, collective resistance, or an exacerbation of mutual divisions and conflicts? Given the complexity of such situations in practice, the question is perhaps somewhat naive; but given the Hobbesian argument so insistently developed throughout this piece, it clearly deserves at least a schematic and provisional answer here.[117]

Two key variables can be said to affect the likely result of the encounter (Figure 1). The first is the independent military strength of the foreign power (not including potential local allies). A very weak outsider is neither attractive as an ally for individual parties in the domestic power struggle, nor credible as a means of putting an end to that struggle by helping to enforce a common peace. An alien group with too much independent military capability, on the other hand, is likely to be distrusted as a dangerous ally and a potentially oppressive ruler (although of course it may use its strength to impose its rule unilaterally). The second major variable, represented here on the vertical axis, is the extent to which the outside power is seen or believed to act with impartiality in its dealings with the various indigenous polities. Very impartial outsiders may be welcomed as arbiters of the peace even if their ability to enforce it is slight, and attractive as enforcers of the peace even if they are dangerously strong. Conversely, an outside power which – whether due to lack of foresight and political skill, or to existing ties with particular local actors – is unable not to choose sides in domestic disputes will be attractive only as an ally for those parties which it favours, and that only if it is strong enough to provide them with useful support; too strong, moreover, and it may instill in them a prohibitive fear of permanent domination, or decide it has no need of their help anyway. Other things being equal, the impartiality of a more obviously foreign or reputedly sacred external power – in the past, the two qualities often went together – will tend to be more credible than that of a relatively familiar and mundane one. A reputation for impartiality, however, can also be based on observed judicial performance in practice, which depends on political disinterestedness and/or commitment to impersonal justice.

In drawing attention to the conflict-ridden character of many stateless societies and their consequent vulnerability to, or even enthusiasm for, colonial expansion, it is not my intention to idealise colonial rulers or their motives. During the period of very heavy compulsory labour services in the nineteenth century, Dutch officials in Minahasa shocked even some European visitors with the single-minded way in which they 'abused their superior position to appropriate the fruits of the sweat and toil of many thousands of their minions' (Dumont d'Ur-

---

117 Figure 1 is intended strictly as a suggestive model; I have not attempted to locate on the diagram the specific historical situations and outcomes described above.

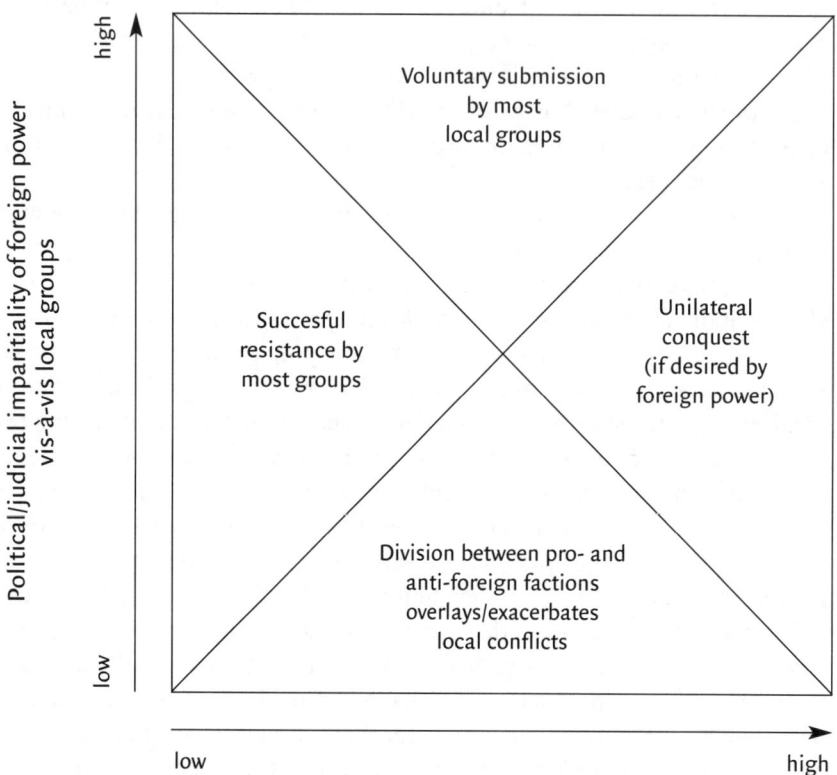

Figure 1 *Likely outcomes of interaction between a foreign power and a set of mutually hostile local groups*

ville 1833: 444).[118] Nor do I mean to provide an apology for the behaviour of missionaries like Adriani and Kruyt, who, after more than a decade of fruitless preaching to an uncolonised people, decided that the Christianisation of the Toraja would have to be 'less a spiritual than a political process' (Arts 1986: 111) and concluded an unholy alliance with colonial arms which in due course enabled them to reap a famous evangelical success in the aftermath of a military

---

[118] Unfortunately others, including the much-quoted Alfred Russel Wallace (1987: 194-7), were less critical.

CONCLUDING REMARKS

conquest.[119] Nor, perhaps most importantly, do I suppose that the stateless societies of Indonesia were any more violent, fissiparous or fragile than their counterparts elsewhere in the world. Yet we will not understand the nature of those societies better if, whether out of embarrassment, disbelief, or lack of interest, we choose to ignore either the ease with which they were often brought under colonial control, or the evidence that 'stranger-kings' were perceived as fulfilling useful functions among them. By focusing on the indigenous roots of colonialism, we may also acquire a more realistic awareness of the obstacles to peaceful cooperation in Indonesian (and other) societies and a clearer perception of the usefulness of states in overcoming these. In Indonesia as elsewhere, the real challenge for the future is not to do without the state, nor even to weaken it, but rather to tame it in such a way that it provides a high quality of justice while giving as little cause as possible for jealousy.

---

119 In the testimony of A.J.N. Engelenberg (1906: 14), the colonial administrator who presided over the military conquest of the Toraja in 1905-7: 'To reject the use of force *a priori*, purely out of distaste for violence, is unhealthy. The evangelists themselves request it [...]'.

Abbreviations

ANRI Manado	Arsip Nasional Republik Indonesia (Jakarta), Arsip Manado
ANRI Gorontalo	Arsip Nasional Republik Indonesia (Jakarta), Arsip Gorontalo
ARA ASB	Algemeen Rijksarchief (Den Haag), Archief van de Algemene Secretarie te Batavia
ARA MvO	Algemeen Rijksarchief (Den Haag), Memories van Overgave
ARA VOC	Algemeen Rijksarchief (Den Haag), VOC Overgekomen Brieven en Papieren
AV	Algemeen/Administratief Verslag
CD	Corpus Diplomaticum (see bibliography)
GM	Generale Missiven (see bibliography)
KITLV HS	Koninklijk Instituut voor Taal-, Land- en Volkenkunde (Leiden), Westerse Handschriften
KV	Koloniaal Verslag (see bibliography)
Res.	Resident (colonial official in charge of a residency)
VKI	Verhandelingen van het Koninklijk Instituut (KITLV)

Bibliography

Aa, Robidé van der (ed.) (1867) 'Het journaal van Padtbrugge's reis naar Noord-Celebes en de Noordereilanden. (16 Aug.-23 Dec. 1677.)', *Bijdragen tot de Taal-, Land- en Volkenkunde van Nederlandsch-Indië* 14: 105-565.
Acheson, James M. (ed.) (1994) *Anthropology and institutional economics*. Lanham, Maryland: University Press of America. [Monographs in Economic Anthropology 12.]
Adas, Michael (1981) 'From avoidance to confrontation: peasant protest in precolonial and colonial Southeast Asia', *Comparative Studies in Society and History* 23: 217-47.
Adas, Michael (1993) '"High" imperialism and the "New" History', in: Michael Adas (ed.), *Islamic and European expansion; The forging of a global order*, pp. 311-44. Philadelphia: Temple University Press.
Adriani, N. (1901a) 'De invloed van Loewoe op Midden-Celebes', *Mededeelingen van wege het Nederlandsch Zendelinggenootschap* 45: 153-64.
Adriani, N. (1901b) 'Mededeelingen omtrent de Toradjas van Midden-Celebes; lezing gehouden door Dr. N. Adriani den 3en September 1900', *Tijdschrift voor Indische Taal-, Land- en Volkenkunde* 44: 215-54.
Adriani, N. (1913) 'Verhaal der ontdekkingsreis van Jhr. J.C.W.D.A. van der Wyck naar het Posso-Meer, 16-22 October, 1865', *De Indische Gids* 35-2: 843-62.
Adriani, N. (1915) 'Maatschappelijke, speciaal economische verandering der bevolking van Midden-Celebes, sedert de invoering van het Nederlandsch gezag aldaar', *Tijdschrift van het Koninklijk Nederlandsch Aardrijkskundig Genootschap* (2nd series) 32: 457-75.
Adriani, N. (1916) 'De Hoofden der Toradja's in Midden-Celebes', *Indisch Genootschap; Verslagen der Algemeene Vergaderingen* 1915/16: 107-26.
Adriani, N. (1917) 'De Toradja'sche vrouw als priesteres', *Verslagen en Mededeelingen der Koninklijke Akademie van Wetenschappen, Afdeeling Letterkunde* 5-2: 453-78.
Adriani, N. [1919] *Poso (Midden-Celebes)*. Den Haag: Zendingsstudie-raad. [Onze Zendingsvelden II.]
Adriani, N. (1921) *Korte schets van het Toradja-volk in Midden-Celebes*. Oegstgeest: Zendingsbureau.

Adriani, N. (1932) [1915] 'Over het karakter der Toradja's en hunne rechtspraak', in: *Verzamelde geschriften van Dr. N. Adriani*, Vol. 2, pp. 25-49. Haarlem: De Erven F. Bohn.

Adriani, N., and Alb.C. Kruyt (1900) 'Van Posso naar Mori, 22 Augustus-29 September 1899', *Mededeelingen van wege het Nederlandsch Zendelinggenootschap* 44: 135-214.

Adriani, N., and Alb.C. Kruyt (1912-14) *De Bare'e-sprekende Toradja's van Midden-Celebes*. Batavia: Landsdrukkerij. 3 vols.

Adriani, N., and Alb.C. Kruyt (1950-51) *De Bare'e sprekende Toradjas van Midden-Celebes (de Oost-Toradjas)*. Amsterdam: Noord-Hollandsche. 3 vols.

Alders, L.W. (1955) *Internationale rechtspraak tussen Indonesische rijken en de V.O.C. tot 1700*. Nijmegen: Centrale Drukkerij.

Andaya, Barbara Watson (1993) *To live as brothers; Southeast Sumatra in the seventeenth and eighteenth centuries*. Honolulu: Hawaii University Press.

Andaya, Leonard Y. (1978) 'Treaty conceptions and misconceptions: a case study from South Sulawesi', *Bijdragen tot de Taal-, Land- en Volkenkunde* 134: 275-95.

Andaya, Leonard Y. (1981) *The heritage of Arung Palakka; A history of South Sulawesi (Celebes) in the seventeenth century*. The Hague: Martinus Nijhoff. [VKI 91.]

Andaya, Leonard Y. (1993) *The world of Maluku; Eastern Indonesia in the early modern period*. Honolulu: University of Hawaii Press.

Andrade, Tonio (1997) 'Political spectacle and colonial rule; the landdag on Dutch Taiwan, 1629-1648', *Itinerario* 21: 57-93.

Angerler, Johann (1995) [review of] Masashi Hirosue, *Prophets and followers in Batak millenarian responses to the colonial order* [Canberra 1988], *Bijdragen tot de Taal-, Land- en Volkenkunde* 151: 136-8.

Aragon, Lorraine V. (1992) *Divine justice: Cosmology, ritual, and Protestant missionization in Central Sulawesi, Indonesia*. PhD thesis, University of Illinois at Urbana-Champaign (reproduced Ann Arbor, Michigan: University Microfilms International, 1993).

Aragon, Lorraine V. (2000) *Fields of the Lord; Animism, Christian minorities, and state development in Indonesia*. Honolulu: University of Hawaii Press.

Arts, J.A. (1986) 'Zending en bestuur op Midden-Celebes tussen 1890 en 1920; samenwerking, confrontatie en eigen verantwoordelijkheid', in: J. van Goor (ed.), *Imperialisme in de marge; De afronding van Nederlands-Indië*, pp. 85-121. Utrecht: HES.

Axelrod, Robert (1990) [1984] *The evolution of cooperation*. London: Penguin.

Banfield, Edward C. (1958) *The moral basis of a backward society*. Glencoe, Illinois: The Free Press.

Barlow, Colin (ed.) (1999) *Institutions and economic change in Southeast Asia; The context of development from the 1960s to the 1990s*. Cheltenham: Edward Elgar.

Barton, R.F. (1938) *Philippine pagans; The autobiographies of three Ifugaos*. London: George Routledge.

Barton, R.F. (1949) *The Kalingas; Their institutions and custom law*. Chicago: University of Chicago Press.

Barton, R.F. (1969) [1919] *Ifugao law*. Berkeley: University of California Press.

Bastiaans, J. (1938) 'Het verbond tusschen Limbotto en Gorontalo', *Tijdschrift voor Indische Taal-, Land- en Volkenkunde* 78: 215-47.
Bastiaans, J. (1939) 'Batato's in het oude Gorontalo, in verband met den Gorontaleeschen staatsbouw', *Tijdschrift voor Indische Taal-, Land- en Volkenkunde* 79: 23-72.
Bates, Robert H. (1983) *Essays on the political economy of rural Africa*. Cambridge: Cambridge University Press.
Beck, W.J. (1922) 'Mapaloes', *Koloniale Studiën* 6: 64-8.
Blair, Emma H., and J.A. Robertson (1902) *The Philippine Islands, 1493-1898* [...], Vol. 2. Cleveland, Ohio: Arthur H. Clark.
Bleeker, P. (1856) *Reis door de Minahassa en den Molukschen archipel, gedaan in de maanden September en October 1855*. Batavia: Lange.
Bloodworth, Dennis (1975) *An eye for the dragon; South-east Asia observed, 1954-73*. Harmondsworth, Middlesex: Penguin.
Blussé, J.L., M.E. van Opstall and Ts'ao Yung-Ho (eds) (1986) *De dagregisters van het kasteel Zeelandia, Taiwan 1629-1662; Deel I: 1629-1641*. 's-Gravenhage: Martinus Nijhoff. [Rijks Geschiedkundige Publicatiën, Grote Serie 195.]
Bouvy, A.C.N. (1924) 'Uit en over de Minahasa. I. De Minahassa en de geneeskunst', *Bijdragen tot de Taal-, Land- en Volkenkunde van Nederlandsch-Indië* 80: 365-96.
Bowen, John R. (1986) 'On the political construction of tradition; gotong royong in Indonesia', *Journal of Asian Studies* 45: 545-61.
Bronson, Bennet (1977) 'Exchange at the upstream and downstream ends: notes toward a functional model of the coastal state in Southeast Asia', in: Karl L. Hutterer (ed.), *Economic exchange and social interaction in Southeast Asia: Perspectives from prehistory, history, and ethnography*, pp. 39-52. Ann Arbor: The University of Michigan Center for South and Southeast Asian Studies. [Michigan Papers on South and Southeast Asia 13.]
Buddingh, S.A. (1860) *Neêrlands-Oost-Indie; Reizen over Java, Madura, Makasser, Saleijer, Bima, Menado, Sangier eilanden, Talau-eilanden, Ternate* [...]. Vol. 2. Rotterdam: M. Wijt.
Bullbeck, David, and Ian Caldwell (2000) *Land of iron; The historical archaeology of Luwu and the Cenrana valley*. Hull: Centre for South-East Asian Studies, University of Hull.
Campbell, William (1903) *Formosa under the Dutch; Described from contemporary records with explanatory notes and a bibliography of the island*. London: Kegan Paul, Trench, Trubner.
Caplan, Gerald L. (1969) 'Barotseland's scramble for protection', *Journal of African History* 10: 277-94.
Chabot, H.Th. (1950) *Verwantschap, stand en sexe in Zuid-Celebes*. Groningen: J.B. Wolters. [PhD thesis, Balai Perguruan Tinggi Republik Indonesia.]
Chabot, H.Th. (1969) 'Processes of change in Siau 1890-1950', *Bijdragen tot de Taal-, Land- en Volkenkunde* 125: 94-102.
Clercq, F.S.A. de (1870a) 'Boekaankondiging', *Tijdschrift voor Nederlandsch Indië* 1870-1: 124-37.
Clercq, F.S.A. de (1870b) 'Iets over het bijgeloof in de Minahasa', *Tijdschrift voor Nederlandsch Indië* 1870-2: 1-11.

Clercq, F.S.A. de (1883) 'Schets van het landschap Bolaäng-Mongondow', *Tijdschrift van het Koninklijk Nederlandsch Aardrijkskundig Genootschap* (2nd series) 7: 116-25.

Colenbrander, H.T. (1898) 'Officiele berichten omtrent het opheffen van den Compagnie's post te Parigi', *Mededeelingen van wege het Nederlandsch Zendelinggenootschap* 42: 587-95.

Colin, Francisco (1900) [1660] *Labor evangelica ministerios apostolicos de los obreros de la Compañia de Iesus, fundacion, y progressos de su provincia en las Islas Filipinas*, Vol. 1. Barcelona: Henrich y Compañia. [Pablo Pastells, ed.]

Colson, Elizabeth (1966) 'The alien diviner and local politics among the Tonga of Zambia', in: Marc J. Swartz, Victor W. Turner and Arthur Tuden (eds), *Political anthropology*, pp. 221-8. Chicago: Aldine Atherton.

Coolsma, S. (1893) 'De zending op de Sangir- en Talaut-eilanden', *Nederlandsch Zendingstijdschrift* 5: 193-298.

Corpus Diplomaticum (1907-55) *Corpus Diplomaticum Nederlando-Indicum*. 's-Gravenhage: Martinus Nijhoff. 6 vols. [J.E. Heeres and F.W. Stapel, eds.]

Crab, P. van der (1875) *Memorie van overgave van de residentie Menado*. [ARA MvO MMK 229.]

Crawfurd, John (1820) *History of the Indian Archipelago. Containing an account of the manners, arts, languages, religions, institutions, and commerce of its inhabitants*. Edinburgh: Archibald Constable. 3 vols.

Cuarteron, D. Carlo (1855) *Spiegazione e traduzione dei XIV quadri relativi alle isole di Salibaboo, Talaor, Sanguey, Nanuse, Mindanao, Celebes, Bornèo, Bahalatolis, Tambisan, Sulu, Toolyan, e Labuan presentati alla sacra congregatione de propaganda fide nel mese di Settembre 1852*. Roma: Tipografia della S.C. di Propaganda Fide.

Dagh-Register (1919) [1681] *Dagh-Register gehouden int Casteel Batavia [...]*. Batavia: Landsdrukkerij. [F. de Haan, ed.]

Dam, Pieter van (1931) [1701] *Beschrijving van de Oostindische Compagnie*, Vol. 2-1. 's-Gravenhage: Martinus Nijhoff. [Rijks Geschiedkundige Publicatiën 74; F.W. Stapel, ed.]

[Delden, A.J. van] (1844) 'De Sangir-eilanden in 1825', *Indisch Magazijn* 1 (4-6): 356-383; 1 (7-9): 1-32.

Dewey, Alice G. (1962) *Peasant marketing in Java*. New York: The Free Press of Glencoe.

Dobbin, Christine (1975) 'The exercise of authority in Minangkabau in the late eighteenth century', in: Anthony Reid and Lance Castles (eds), *Pre-colonial state systems in Southeast Asia*, pp. 77-89. Kuala Lumpur: Malaysian Branch of the Royal Asiatic Society. [MBRAS Monograph 6.]

Dobbin, Christine (1983) *Islamic revivalism in a changing peasant economy; Central Sumatra, 1784-1847*. London: Curzon Press. [Scandinavian Institute of Asian Studies Monograph Series 47.]

Doren, J.B.J. van (1860) *Herinneringen en schetsen van Nederlands Oost-Indië*, Vol. 2. Amsterdam: J.D. Sybrandi.

Downs, Richard Erskine (1955) 'Head-hunting in Indonesia', Bijdragen tot de Taal-, Land- en Volkenkunde 111: 40-70.
Drakard, Jane (1999) A kingdom of words; Language and power in Sumatra. Kuala Lumpur: Oxford University Press.
Dozier, Edward P. (1966) Mountain arbiters; The changing life of a Philippine hill people. Tucson: The University of Arizona Press.
Drobak, John N., and John V.C. Nye (eds) (1997) The frontiers of the new institutional economics. San Diego: Academic Press.
Dumia, Mariano A. (1979) The Ifugao world. Quezon City: New Day.
Dumont d'Urville, M.J. (1833) Voyage de la corvette l'Astrolabe exécuté par ordre du Roi, pendant les années 1826-1827-1828-1829 [...], Vol. 5. Paris: J. Tastu.
Dunnebier, W. (1949) 'Over de vorsten van Bolaang Mongondow', Bijdragen tot de Taal-, Land- en Volkenkunde 105: 219-74.
Edeling, A.C.J. (1919) [1875] 'Memorie omtrent de Minahasa, uitgebracht door den in 1874 bij gouvernementsbesluit met een zending naar Menado belasten hoofdambtenaar op nonactiviteit A.C.J. Edeling (1875)', Adatrechtbundel 17: 5-95.
Elster, Jon (1989) Solomonic judgements; Studies in the limitations of rationality. Cambridge: Cambridge University Press.
Evans-Pritchard, E.E. (1940) The Nuer; A description of the modes of livelihood and political institutions of a Nilotic people. Oxford: Clarendon.
Evans-Pritchard, E.E. (1976) [1937] Witchcraft, oracles, and magic among the Azande. Oxford: Clarendon Press. [Eva Gillies, ed.]
Fernández-Armesto, Felipe (2000) 'The stranger-effect in early modern Asia', Itinerario 24-2: 80-103.
Foster, Brian L. (1977) 'Trade, social conflict and social interaction; rethinking some old ideas on exchange', in: Karl L. Hutterer (ed.), Economic exchange and social interaction in Southeast Asia; perspectives from prehistory, history, and ethnography, pp. 3-22. Ann Arbor: Center for South and Southeast Asian Studies, University of Michigan. [Michigan Papers on South and Southeast Asia 13.]
Foster, George M. (1965) 'Peasant society and the image of limited good', American Anthropologist 67: 293-315.
Fox, James J. (1977) Harvest of the palm; Ecological change in eastern Indonesia. Cambridge, Massachusetts: Harvard University Press.
Fox, James J. (1995) 'Austronesian societies and their transformations', in: Peter Bellwood, James J. Fox and Darrell Tryon (eds), The Austronesians: Historical and comparative perspectives, pp. 214-28. Canberra: Department of Anthropology, Research School of Pacific and Asian Studies, Australian National University.
Fragment (1856) 'Fragment uit een reisverhaal', Tijdschrift voor Nederlandsch Indië 1856-1: 391-432; 1856-2: 1-38, 69-100, 141-60.
Francis, E. (1860) Herinneringen uit den levensloop van een' Indisch' ambtenaar van 1815 tot 1851, Vol. 3. Batavia: H.M. van Dorp.

Frieswijck, E. (1902) 'Aanteekeningen betreffende den geografischen en ethnografischen toestand van het eiland Tagoelandang (Afdeeling Sangi- en Talaut-eilanden)', *Tijdschrift voor het Binnenlandsch Bestuur* 22: 426-38, 469-89.

Gallois, W.O. (1892) *Rapport nopens den staat van zaken in de Minahassa*. Batavia: Landsdrukkerij.

Gellner, Ernest (1995) 'The importance of being modular', in: John A. Hall (ed.), *Civil society; Theory, history, comparison*, pp. 32-55. Cambridge: Polity Press.

Generale Missiven (1960-97) *Generale missiven van gouverneurs-generaal en raden aan Heren XVII der Verenigde Oostindische Compagnie*. 's-Gravenhage: Martinus Nijhoff / Bureau der Rijkscommissie voor Vaderlandse Geschiedenis / Instituut voor Nederlandse Geschiedenis. 11 vols. [W.Ph. Coolhaas, J. van Goor and J.E. Schooneveld-Oosterling, eds.]

Gluckman, Max (1965) *Politics, law and ritual in tribal society*. Oxford: Basil Blackwell.

Godée Molsbergen, E.C. (1928) *Geschiedenis van de Minahassa tot 1829*. Weltevreden: Landsdrukkerij.

Goedhart, O.H. (1908) 'Drie landschappen in Celebes', *Tijdschrift voor Indische Taal-, Land- en Volkenkunde* 50: 442-548.

Graafland, N. (1864) 'Fragment eener onuitgegevene beschrijving van de Minahassa', *Mededeelingen van wege het Nederlandsch Zendelinggenootschap* 8: 1-23.

Graafland, N. (1867-69) *De Minahassa. Haar verleden en haar tegenwoordige toestand*. Rotterdam: M. Wijt. 2 vols.

Greif, Avner (1998) 'Self-enforcing political systems and economic growth: late medieval Genoa', in: Robert H. Bates, Avner Greif, Margaret Levi, Jean-Laurent Rosenthal and Barry R. Weingast, *Analytic narratives*, pp. 23-63. Princeton, New Jersey: Princeton University Press.

Gullick, J.M. (1958) *Indigenous political systems of western Malaya*. London: The Athlone Press. [London School of Economics Monographs on Social Anthropology 17.]

Hall, D.G.E. (1968) *A history of South-East Asia* (3rd edition). London: MacMillan.

Hart, C. van der (1853) *Reize rondom het eiland Celebes en naar eenige der Moluksche eilanden*. 's-Gravenhage: K. Fuhri.

Harvey, Barbara S. (1977) *Permesta: half a rebellion*. Ithaca, New York: Cornell Modern Indonesia Project, Southeast Asia Program, Cornell University. [Monograph Series 57.]

Hefner, Robert W. (2000) *Civil Islam; Muslims and democratization in Indonesia*. Princeton: Princeton University Press.

Hekker, M. (1987) 'Mapalus in Nederland; cultuurherstel onder Minahassische immigranten', *Bijdragen tot de Taal-, Land- en Volkenkunde* 143: 104-24.

Henley, David (1993) 'A superabundance of centers: Ternate and the contest for North Sulawesi', *Cakalele; Maluku Research Journal* 4: 39-60.

Henley, David (1996) *Nationalism and regionalism in a colonial context; Minahasa in the Dutch East Indies*. Leiden: KITLV Press. [VKI 168.]

Henley, David (1997) 'Goudkoorts; mijnbouw, gezondheid en milieu op Sulawesi (1670-1995), *Spiegel Historiael* 32: 424-30.

Henley, David [in press] *Fertility, food and fever; Population, economy and environment in North and Central Sulawesi, 1600-1930.* Leiden: KITLV Press.

Hirschman, Albert O. (1958) *The strategy of economic development.* New Haven: Yale University Press.

Hissink, [C.] (1912) 'Nota van toelichting, betreffende de zelfbesturende landschappen Paloe, Dolo, Sigi en Beromaroe', *Tijdschrift voor Indische Taal-, Land- en Volkenkunde* 54: 58-128.

Hobbes, Thomas (1996) [1651] *Leviathan.* Cambridge: Cambridge university Press. [Richard Tuck, ed.]

Jacobs, Els M. (2000) *Koopman in Azië; De handel van de Verenigde Oost-Indische Compagnie tijdens de 18de eeuw.* Zutphen: Walburg.

Jacobs, H. (ed.) (1974-84) *Documenta Malucensia.* Roma: Institutum Historicum Societatis Iesu. 3 vols.

Jenista, Frank Lawrence (1987) *The white apos; American governors on the Cordillera Central.* Quezon City: New Day.

Josselin de Jong, Patrick Edward de (1951) *Minangkabau and Negri Sembilan; Socio-political structure in Indonesia.* Leiden: Eduard IJdo. [PhD thesis, Rijksuniversiteit Leiden.]

Junker, Laura Lee (1999) *Raiding, trading, and feasting; The political economy of Philippine chiefdoms.* Honolulu: University of Hawaii Press.

Kaudern, Walter (1925) *Structures and settlements in Central Celebes.* Göteborg: Elanders Boktryckeri Aktiebolag. [Ethnographical studies in Celebes; Results of the author's expedition to Celebes 1917-1920, I.]

Keesing, Felix M. and Marie (1934) *Taming Philippine headhunters; A study of government and of cultural change in northern Luzon.* London: George Allen and Unwin.

Kiefer, Thomas M. (1972) *The Tausug; Violence and law in a Philippine Moslem society.* New York: Holt, Rinehart and Winston.

Koentjaraningrat (1961) *Some social-anthropological observations on gotong rojong practices in two villages of Central Java.* Ithaca, New York: Cornell University Modern Indonesia Project.

Koentjaraningrat (1975) *Anthropology in Indonesia; A bibliographical review.* 's-Gravenhage: Martinus Nijhoff. [KITLV Bibliographical Series 8.]

Koloniaal Verslag (1848-1941) [title varies]. 's-Gravenhage.

Korn, B. (1939) *Nota van de onderafdelingen Gorontalo en Boalemo.* [ARA MvO KIT 1199.]

Kruyt, Alb.C. (1892) 'Mijne reis van Gorontalo naar Poso (Posso), met den Gouvernementsstoomer "Zeeduif", 4-16 Februari 1892', *Mededeelingen van wege het Nederlandsch Zendelinggenootschap* 36: 225-56.

Kruyt, Alb.C. (1895) 'Een en ander aangaande het geestelijk en maatschappelijk leven van den Poso-Alfoer, II. Politieke verhoudingen. Standen. Rechtspraak', *Mededeelingen van wege het Nederlandsch Zendelinggenootschap* 39: 106-28.

Kruyt, Alb.C. (1899) 'Het koppensnellen der Toradja's van Midden-Celebes, en zijne beteekenis', *Verslagen en Mededeelingen der Koninklijke Akademie van Wetenschappen, Afdeeling Letterkunde* 4-3: 147-229.

Kruyt, Alb.C. (1900a) 'Eenige ethnografische aanteekeningen omtrent de Toboengkoe en de Tomori', *Mededeelingen van wege het Nederlandsch Zendelinggenootschap* 44: 215-48.

Kruyt, Alb.C. (1900b) 'Het rijk Mori', *Tijdschrift van het Koninklijk Nederlandsch Aardrijkskundig Genootschap* (2nd series) 17: 436-66.

Kruyt, Alb.C. (1901) 'Het ijzer in Midden-Celebes', *Bijdragen tot de Taal-, Land- en Volkenkunde van Nederlandsch-Indië* 53: 148-60.

Kruyt, Alb.C. (1908) 'De berglandschappen Napoe en Besoa in Midden-Celebes', *Tijdschrift van het Koninklijk Nederlandsch Aardrijkskundig Genootschap* (2nd series) 25: 1271-1344.

Kruyt, Alb.C. (1911) 'De slavernij in Posso (Midden-Celebes)', *Onze Eeuw; Maandschrift voor Staatkunde, Letteren, Wetenschap en Kunst* 11-1: 61-97.

Kruyt, Alb.C. [1926] *Van heiden tot Christen*. Oegstgeest: Zendingsbureau.

Kruyt, Alb.C. (1930) 'De To Wana op Oost-Celebes', *Tijdschrift voor Indische Taal-, Land- en Volkenkunde* 70: 397-627.

Kruyt, Alb.C. (1931) 'De vorsten van Banggai', *Koloniaal Tijdschrift* 20: 505-28, 605-23.

Kruyt, Alb.C. (1932a) 'Balantaksche studiën', *Tijdschrift voor Indische Taal-, Land- en Volkenkunde* 72: 328-90.

Kruyt, Alb.C. (1932b) 'De bewoners van den Banggai-archipel', *Tijdschrift van het Koninklijk Nederlandsch Aardrijkskundig Genootschap* (2nd series) 49: 66-88, 249-71.

Kruyt, Alb.C. (1938) *De West-Toradjas op Midden-Celebes*. Amsterdam: Noord-Hollandsche. 4 vols.

Kruyt, Alb.C. and J. (1921) 'Verslag van een reis naar het landschap Napoe in de onderafd. Posso (Celebes)', *Tijdschrift van het Koninklijk Nederlandsch Aardrijkskundig Genootschap* (2nd series) 38: 400-414.

Kruyt, J. (1924) 'De Moriërs van Tinompo (oostelijk Midden-Celebes)', *Bijdragen tot de Taal-, Land- en Volkenkunde van Nederlandsch-Indië* 80: 33-217.

Kruyt, J. (1970) *Het zendingsveld Poso; Geschiedenis van een confrontatie*. Kampen: J.H. Kok.

Laag, C.M. ter (1920) *Nota van overgave van de onderafdeling Donggala*. [ARA MvO KIT 1196.]

Landschap Donggala (1905) 'Het landschap Donggala of Banawa', *Bijdragen tot de Taal-, Land- en Volkenkunde van Nederlandsch-Indië* 58: 514-31.

Lawrence, T.E. (1935) *Seven pillars of wisdon; A triumph*. London: Jonathan Cape.

Li, Tania Murray (2001) 'Relational histories and the production of difference on Sulawesi's upland frontier', *Journal of Asian Studies* 60: 41-66.

Lichbach, Mark Irving (1995) *The rebel's dilemma*. Ann Arbor: The University of Michigan Press.

Lichbach, Mark Irving (1996) *The cooperator's dilemma*. Ann Arbor: The University of Michigan Press.

Locke, John (1963) [1689] *A letter concerning toleration*. The Hague: Martinus Nijhoff. [Mario Montuori, ed.]

Mair, Lucy (1962) *Primitive government*. Harmondsworth, Middlesex: Penguin.

Mambu, Eddy (1986) *Jalannya Perang Tondano*. [Paper presented at the Seminar Perang Tondano, Jakarta, 11.1986.]

Mangindaän, L. (1873) 'Oud Tondano', *Tijdschrift voor Indische Taal-, Land- en Volkenkunde* 20: 364-77.

Matthes, P.A. (1881) *Memorie van overgave van de residentie Menado*. [ARA MvO MMK 300.]

Mauss, Marcel (1969) [1925] *The gift; Forms and functions of exchange in archaic societies*. London: Routledge and Kegan Paul. [Ian Cunnison, transl.; E.E. Evans-Pritchard, ed.]

Menopo, Johannis Manuel (1893) 'Menambahi deri kaoel dan perdjandjian diboeat pengakoewan dan di bertegoehken segala hal-hal diantara oleh akoe Padoeka Radja Johannis Manuel Menopo serta mantri[2] koe jang bergoena sekarang soedah mengakoe dan mengarti hadat[2] di tanah Karadjaan Bolaang Mongondo [...]', *Tijdschrift voor Indische Taal-, Land- en Volkenkunde* 35: 481-97.

Metcalfe, G.E. (1962) *Maclean of the Gold Coast; The life and times of George Maclean, 1801-1847*. London: Oxford University Press.

Meyer, A.B., and O. Richter (1903) *Celebes I: Sammlung der Herren Dr. Paul und Dr. Fritz Sarasin aus den Jahren 1893-1896*. Dresden: Stengel. [Publikationen aus dem Königlichen Ethnographischen Museum zu Dresden 14.]

Miller, Gary, and Kathleen Cook (1998) 'Leveling and leadership: hierarchy and social order', in: Karol Soltan, Eric M. Uslaner and Virginia Haufler (eds), *Institutions and social order*, pp. 67-100. Ann Arbor: University of Michigan Press.

Molander, Per (1992) 'The prevalence of free riding', *Journal of Conflict Resolution* 36: 756-71.

Nes, P. de (1925) 'Het onderwijs aan inlanders in de Minahassa', *Bijdragen tot de Taal-, Land- en Volkenkunde van Nederlandsch-Indië* 81: 500-522.

Newson, Linda A. (1998) 'Old World diseases in the early colonial Philippines and Spanish America', in: Daniel F. Doeppers and Peter Xenos (eds), *Population and history; The demographic origins of the modern Philippines*, pp. 17-36. Madison, Wisconsin: Center for Southeast Asian Studies, University of Wisconsin-Madison.

Niemeijer, H.E. (ed.) [forthcoming] *Memories van overgave van gouverneurs van de Molukken (Ternate) in de zeventiende en achttiende eeuw*.

Northrup, David (1978) *Trade without rulers; Pre-colonial economic development in South-Eastern Nigeria*. Oxford: Oxford University Press.

Nourse, Jennifer W. (1999) *Conceiving spirits; Birth rituals and contested identities among Laujé of Indonesia*. Washington: Smithsonian Institution Press.

Nur, Samin Rajik (1979) *Beberapa aspek hukum adat tatanegara kerajaan Gorontalo pada masa pemerintahan Eato (1673-1679)*. [PhD thesis, Universitas Hasanuddin, Ujung Pandang.]

Olivier, J. (1837) Reizen in den Molukschen archipel naar Makassar, enz. in het gevolg van den gouverneur-generaal van Nederland's Indië, in 1824 gedaan, Vol. 2. Amsterdam: G.J.A. Beijerinck.
Oosten, Jarich G. (1988) 'The stranger-king; a problem of comparison', in: Henri J.M. Claessen and David S. Moyer (eds), Time past, time present, time future; Perspectives on Indonesian culture; Essays in honour of Professor P.E. de Josselin de Jong, pp. 259-75. Dordrecht: Foris. [VKI 131.]
Ottenberg, Simon (1958) 'Ibo oracles and intergroup relations', Southwestern Journal of Antthropology 14: 295-317.
Pabbruwe, H.J. [1994] Dr Robertus Padtbrugge (Parijs 1637-Amersfoort 1703), dienaar van de Verenigde Oost-Indische Compagnie, en zijn familie. Kloosterzande: Duerinck.
Padtbrugge, Robert (1866) [1679] 'Beschrijving der zeden en gewoonten van de bewoners der Minahassa', Bijdragen tot de Taal-, Land- en Volkenkunde van Nederlandsch-Indië 13: 304-31.
Pagden, Anthony (1988) 'The destruction of trust and its economic consequences in the case of eighteenth-century Naples', in: Diego Gambetta (ed.), Trust; Making and breaking cooperative relations, pp. 127-41. Oxford: Basil Blackwell.
Pelras, C. (1996) The Bugis. Oxford: Blackwell.
Phelan, John Leddy (1959) The Hispanization of the Philippines; Spanish aims and Filipino responses, 1565-1700. Madison: The University of Wisconsin Press.
Poundstone, William (1992) Prisoner's dilemma. New York: Doubleday.
Pringle, Robert (1970) Rajahs and rebels; The Ibans of Sarawak under Brooke rule, 1841-1941. London: Macmillan.
Ptak, Roderich (1992) 'The northern trade route to the spice islands: South China Sea-Sulu Zone-North Moluccas (14th to early 16th century)', Archipel 43: 27-55.
Reid, Anthony (1983) 'Introduction: slavery and bondage in Southeast Asian history', in: Anthony Reid (ed.), Slavery, bondage and dependency in Southeast Asia, pp. 1-43. St. Lucia: University of Queensland Press.
Reid, Anthony (1988-93) Southeast Asia in the age of commerce, 1450-1680. New Haven: Yale University Press. 2 vols.
Reid, Anthony (1997) 'Inside out; the colonial displacement of Sumatra's population', in: Peter Boomgaard, Freek Colombijn and David Henley (eds), Paper landscapes; Explorations in the environmental history of Indonesia, pp. 61-89. Leiden: KITLV Press. [VKI 178.]
Reid, Anthony (1998a) 'Merdeka: the concept of freedom in Indonesia', in: David Kelly and Anthony Reid (eds), Asian freedoms; The idea of freedom in East and Southeast Asia, pp. 141-60. Cambridge: Cambridge University Press.
Reid, Anthony (1998b) 'Political "tradition" in Indonesia: the one and the many', Asian Studies Review 22: 23-38
Reinwardt, C.J.C. (1858) Reis naar het oostelijk gedeelte van den Indischen Archipel, in het jaar 1821. Amsterdam: Frederik Muller. [W.H. de Vriese, ed.]

Renwarin, P.R. (2000) *Matuari wo tonaas Minaesa; Dinamika budaya Tombulu di Minahasa.* [Draft PhD thesis, Leiden University.]

Rhijn, L.J. van (1851) *Reis door den Indischen Archipel, in het belang der evangelische zending.* Rotterdam: M. Wijt.

Ricklefs, M.C. (1974) *Jogjakarta under Sultan Mangkubumi 1749-1792; A history of the division of Java.* London: Oxford University Press.

Ridley, Matt (1996) *The origins of virtue.* London: Viking Penguin.

Riedel, J.G.F. (1862) *Artinja pada menjatakan babarapa perkara deri pada hhikajatnja tuwah tanah Minahasa sampej pada kadatangan orang kulit putih Nederlanda itu.* Batavia: Landsdrukkerij. [Inilah Pintu Gerbang Pengatahuwan itu Apatah Dibukakan Guna Orang-orang Padudokh Tanah Minahasa ini, 5.]

Riedel, J.G.F. (1864a) 'Bijdrage tot de geschiedenis der zeerooverijen op de kusten der Minahasa. [1776 en 1777]', *Tijdschrift voor Indische Taal-, Land- en Volkenkunde* 14: 511-23.

Riedel, J.G.F. (1864b) 'De eedaflegging bij de Tooe-oen-boeloe in de Minahasa', *Tijdschrift voor Indische Taal-, Land- en Volkenkunde* 14: 369-74.

Riedel, J.G.F. (1864c) 'Het landschap Bolaäng-Mongondouw', *Tijdschrift voor Indische Taal-, Land- en Volkenkunde* 13: 266-84.

Riedel, J.G.F. (1870a) 'De landschappen Holontalo, Limoeto, Bone, Boalemo en Kattinggola, of Andagile, geographische, statistische, historische en ethnographische aanteekeningen', *Tijdschrift voor Indische Taal-, Land- en Volkenkunde* 19: 46-153.

Riedel, J.G.F. (1870b) 'De vestiging der Mandaren in de Tomini-landen', *Tijdschrift voor Indische Taal-, Land- en Volkenkunde* 19: 555-64.

Riedel, J.G.F. (1872) [1825] 'De Minahasa in 1825. Bijdrage tot de kennis van Noord-Selebes', *Tijdschrift voor Indische Taal-, Land- en Volkenkunde* 18: 458-568.

Rijkje Mongondo (1880) 'Het rijkje Mongondo en zijn radja', *De Indische Gids* 2-2: 130-31.

Robinson, Ronald (1972) 'Non-European foundations of European imperialism: sketch for a theory of collaboration', in: Roger Owen and Bob Sutcliffe (eds), *Studies in the theory of imperialism,* pp. 117-42. London: Longman.

Robson, Stuart (ed.) (1995) *Desawarnana (Nagarakrtagama) by Mpu Prapanca.* Leiden: KITLV Press. [VKI 169.]

Roorda van Eysinga, S. [1831] *Verschillende reizen en lotgevallen van S. Roorda van Eysinga [...].* Kampen: P.P. Roorda van Eysinga.

Rosaldo, Renato (1980) *Ilonggot headhunting 1883-1974; A study in society and history.* Stanford, California: Stanford University Press.

Sahlins, Marshall D. (1965) 'On the sociology of primitive exchange', in: Michael Banton (ed.), *The relevance of models for social anthropology,* pp. 139-86. London: Tavistock.

Sahlins, Marshall D. (1968) *Tribesmen.* Englewood Cliffs, New Jersey: Prentice-Hall.

Sahlins, Marshall D. (1972) *Stone age economics.* Chicago: Aldine Atherton.

Sahlins, Marshall D. (1985) *Islands of history.* Chicago: University of Chicago Press.

Sarasin, Paul and Fritz (1905) *Reisen in Celebes ausgeführt in den Jahren 1893-1896 und 1902-1903.* Wiesbaden: C.W. Kriedel's Verlag. 2 vols.

Scammell, G.V. (1980) 'Indigenous assistance in the establishment of Portuguese power in Asia in the sixteenth century', *Modern Asian Studies* 14: 1-11.
Schefold, Reimar (1995) 'The heroic theft: myth and achievement in Minahasan society', in: Reimar Schefold (ed.), *Minahasa past and present; Tradition and transition in an outer island region of Indonesia*, pp. 22-31. Leiden: Research School CNWS.
Scherius, R. (1847) 'Eenige bijdragen tot de kennis en den toestand der afdeeling Gorongtalo (eiland Celebes)', *Verhandelingen en Berigten betrekkelijk het Zeewezen en de Zeevaartkunde* (2nd series) 7: 399-421.
Schouten, Mieke J.C. (1988) 'The Minahasans; eternal rivalry', in: N. de Jonge, V. Dekker and R. Schefod (eds), *Indonesia in focus*, pp. 116-21. Meppel: Edu'Actief.
Schouten, Mieke J.C. (1992) 'Heads for force: on the headhunting complex in Southeast Asia and Melanesia', *Anais Universitários, Universitade da Beira Interior, Série Ciências Socias e Humanas* 3: 113-28.
Schouten, Mieke J.C. (1995) 'Wa'ilan and bos: status seeking in Minahasa', in: Reimar Schefold (ed.), *Minahasa past and present; Tradition and transition in an outer island region of Indonesia*, pp. 7-21. Leiden: Research School CNWS.
Schouten, Mieke J.C. (1998) *Leadership and social mobility in a Southeast Asian society; Minahasa, 1677-1983*. Leiden: KITLV Press. [VKI 179.]
Schrauwers, Albert (1997) 'Houses, hierarchy, headhunting and exchange; rethinking political relations in the Southeast Asian realm of Luwu', *Bijdragen tot de Taal-, Land- en Volkenkunde* 153: 356-80.
Schrauwers, Albert (2000) *Colonial 'reformation' in the highlands of Central Sulawesi, Indonesia, 1892-1995*. Toronto: University of Toronto Press.
Schulte Nordholt, Henk (2000) *Een staat van geweld*. [Rede uitgesproken bij de openbare aanvaarding van het ambt van bijzonder hoogleraar in de geschiedenis van Azië, Erasmus Universiteit Rotterdam, 22 juni 2000.]
Schwarz, J. Alb. and A. de Lange (1876) 'De landweg uit de Minahassa naar Bolaäng-Mongondou', *Mededeelingen van wege het Nederlandsch Zendelinggenootschap* 20: 145-79.
Scott, James C. (1998a) 'Freedom and freehold: space, people and state simplification in Southeast Asia'. In: David Kelly and Anthony Reid (eds), *Asian freedoms; The idea of freedom in East and Southeast Asia*, pp. 37-64. Cambridge: Cambridge University Press.
Scott, James C. (1998b) *Seeing like a state; How certain schemes to improve the human condition have failed*. New Haven: Yale University Press.
Scott, William Henry (1974) *The discovery of the Igorots; Spanish contacts with the pagans of northern Luzon*. Quezon City: New Day.
Scott, William Henry (1994) *Barangay; Sixteenth-century Philippine culture and society*. Quezon City: Ateneo de Manila University Press.
Simmel, Georg (1908) *Soziologie. Untersuchungen über die Formen der Vergesellschaftung*. Leipzig: Duncker & Humblot.
Southall, Aidan W. (1970) [1954] *Alur society; A study in processes and types of domination*. Nairobi: Oxford University Press.

Steller, E. (1866) De Sangi-archipel. Amsterdam: H. de Hoogh.
Supit, A.H.D. (1929) 'Mapaloes (1926)', Adatrechtbundel 31: 1-9.
Supit, Bert (1986) Minahasa dari amanat Watu Pinawetengan sampai gelora Minawanua. Jakarta: Sinar Harapan.
Supit, Bert [1991] Sejarah Perang Tondano (Perang Minahasa di Tondano). Jakarta: Yayasan Lembaga Penelitian Sejarah dan Masyarakat.
Sutherland, Heather (1995) 'Believing is seeing: perspectives on political power and economic activity in the Malay world 1700-1940, Journal of Southeast Asian Studies 26: 133-46.
Tacco, Richard (1935) Het volk van Gorontalo (historisch, traditioneel, maatschappelijk, cultureel, sociaal, karakteristiek en economisch). Gorontalo: Yo Un Ann.
Tewksbury, William J. (1967) 'The ordeal as a vehicle for divine intervention in medieval Europe', in: Paul Bohannan (ed.), Law and warfare; Studies in the anthropology of conflict, pp. 267-70. Garden City, New York: The Natural History Press.
Tiele, P.A., and J.E. Heeres (eds) (1886-95) Bouwstoffen voor de geschiedenis der Nederlanders in den Maleischen Archipel. 3 vols. 's-Gravenhage: Martinus Nijhoff.
Tooe oen Boeloesch ordalium (1864) 'Een Tooe oen Boeloesch ordalium', Tijdschrift voor Indische Taal-, Land- en Volkenkunde 14: 506-10.
Uhlenbeck, O.A. (1861) 'De Tomori-expeditie in 1856', Mededeelingen betreffende het Zeewezen 1: 1-61.
Ulfers, S. (1868) 'Het Rano-i-Apo gebied en de bevolking van Bolaäng Mogondou', Mededeelingen van wege het Nederlandsch Zendelinggenootschap 12: 1-26.
Urdaneta, Andres de (1837) 'Relacion escrita y presentada al Emperador por Andres de Urdaneta de los sucesos de la armada del Comendador Loaisa, desde 24 de Julio de 1525 hasta el año 1535', in: Martin Fernandez de Navarrete (ed.), Coleccion de los viages y descubrimientos, que hicieron por mar los Españoles desde fines del siglo XV, Vol. V, pp. 401-39. Madrid: Imprenta Nacional.
Veenhuizen, A.C. (1903) 'Aanteekeningen omtrent Bolaäng-Mongondo', Tijdschrift van het Koninklijk Nederlandsch Aardrijkskundig Genootschap (2nd series) 20: 35-74.
Vergouwen, J.C. (1964) [1933] The social organisation and customary law of the Toba-Batak of northern Sumatra. The Hague: Martinus Nijhoff. [KITLV Translation Series 7.]
Von Rosenberg, C.B.H. (1865) Reistogten in de afdeeling Gorontalo, gedaan op last der Nederlandsch Indische Regering. Amsterdam: Frederik Muller.
Vos, Reinout (1993) Gentle Janus, merchant prince; The VOC and the tightrope of diplomacy in the Malay world, 1740-1800. Leiden: KITLV Press. [VKI 157.]
Wagner, Ulla (1972) Colonialism and Iban warfare. Stokholm: n.n.
Wall, James A., and Ann Lynn (1993) 'Mediation; a current review', Journal of Conflict Resolution 37: 160-94.
Wallace, Alfred Russel (1987) [1869] The Malay archipelago; The land of the orang-utan and the bird of paradise [...]. Singapore: Graham Brash.
Warren, James F. (1981) The Sulu zone 1768-1898. Singapore: Singapore University Press.

Watson, C.W. (1992) *Kinship, property and inheritance in Kerinci, Central Sumatra*. Canterbury: Centre for Social Anthropology and Computing / Centre of South-East Asian Studies, University of Kent at Canterbury. [CSAC Monographs 4.]

Watuseke, F.S. (1986) '"Hukum" and other administrative terms in the languages of Minahasa', *Bijdragen tot de Taal-, Land- en Volkenkunde* 142: 315-24.

Watuseke, F.S., and D.E.F. Henley (1994) 'C.C. Predigers verhandeling over het plaatselijk bestuur en de huishouding van de Minahasa in 1804', *Bijdragen tot de Taal-, Land- en Volkenkunde* 150: 357-85.

Waworoentoe, A.L. (1894) 'De oude geschiedenis der Minahasa volgens de legenden en sagen van het volk', *Verhandelingen van het Bataviaasch Genootschap van Kunsten en Wetenschappen* 47: 85-99.

Weitzel, A.W.P. (1883) 'Geschiedkundig overzicht van de expeditie naar Tomorie op Celebes in het jaar 1856', *Bijdragen tot de Taal-, Land-, en Volkenkunde van Nederlandsch-Indië*, special issue for the Sixth International Congress of Orientalists, pp. 35-56.

Wessels, C. (1935) *De katholieke missie in de Molukken, Noord-Celebes en de Sangihe-eilanden gedurende de Spaansche bestuursperiode 1606-1677*. Tilburg: Henri Bergmans.

Wessels, L. (1891) 'De gouvernments-koffiecultuur in de Minahassa, residentie Menado', *Tijdschrift voor Nederlandsch Indië* 20-1: 50-71, 123-46.

Wilken, N.P., and J.A. Schwarz (1867a) 'Het heidendom en de Islam in Bolaang Mongondow', *Mededeelingen van wege het Nederlandsch Zendinggenootschap* 11: 255-83.

Wilken, N.P., and J.A. Schwarz (1867b) 'Allerlei over het land en volk van Bolaäng Mongondou', *Mededeelingen van wege het Nederlandsch Zendinggenootschap* 11: 284-398.

Woensdregt, Jac. (1928) 'De landbouw bij de To Bada' in Midden-Celebes', *Tijdschrift voor Indische Taal-, Land- en Volkenkunde* 68: 125-255.

Woensdregt, Jac. (1930) 'Lijkbezorging bij de To Bada' in Midden Celebes', *Bijdragen tot de Taal-, Land- en Volkenkunde* 86: 572-611.

Wouden, F.A.E. van (1941) 'Mythen en maatschappij in Boeol', *Tijdschrift voor Indische Taal-, Land- en Volkenkunde* 81: 333-410.

Zainal Abidin (1974) 'The I La Galigo epic cycle of South Celebes and its diffusion', *Indonesia* 17: 161-9.

COMPARATIVE ASIAN STUDIES

General editor: Leontine Visser

PUBLICATIONS IN THIS SERIES

1. CONCEPTUALIZING DEVELOPMENT – THE HISTORICAL-SOCIOLOGICAL TRADITION IN DUTCH NON-WESTERN SOCIOLOGY / Otto van den Muyzenberg and Willem Wolters / isbn 90-6765-382-9 39 p.
2. THE SHATTERED IMAGE – CONSTRUCTION AND DECONSTRUCTION OF THE VILLAGE IN COLONIAL ASIA / Jan Breman / isbn 90-6765-383-7 50 p.
3. SEDUCTIVE MIRAGE – THE SEARCH FOR THE VILLAGE COMMUNITY IN SOUTHEAST ASIA / Jeremy Kemp / isbn 90-6765-384-5 47 p.
4. BETWEEN SOVEREIGN DOMAIN AND SERVILE TENURE – THE DEVELOPMENT OF RIGHTS TO LAND IN JAVA, 1780-1870 / Peter Boomgaard / isbn 90-6765-788-6 61 p.
5. LABOUR MIGRATION AND RURAL TRANSFORMATION IN COLONIAL ASIA / Jan Breman / isbn 90-6765-873-4 82 p.
6. LIVING IN DELI: ITS SOCIETY AS IMAGED IN COLONIAL FICTION / Lily E. Clerkx and Wim F. Wertheim / isbn 90-6765-965-X 126 p.
7. STATE, VILLAGE AND RITUAL IN BALI – A HISTORICAL PERSPECTIVE / Henk Schulte Nordholt / isbn 90-5383-023-5 58 p.
8. THE CENTRALITY OF CENTRAL ASIA / Andre Gunder Frank / isbn 90-5383-079-0 68 p.
9. IDEOLOGICAL INNOVATION UNDER MONARCHY – ASPECTS OF LEGITIMATION ACTIVITY IN CONTEMPORARY BRUNEI / G. Braighlinn / isbn 90-5383-091-X 112 p.
10. THE STATE OF BIHAR / Arvind N. Das / isbn 90-5383-135-5 116 p.
11. ON THE PRODUCTION OF KNOWLEDGE – FIELDWORK IN SOUTH GUJARAT, 1971-1990 / Hein Streefkerk / isbn 90-5383-188-6 54 p.
12. COMPARATIVE ESSAYS ON ASIA AND THE WEST / Wim F. Wertheim / isbn 90-5383-196-7 109 p.
13. COLONIAL PRODUCTION IN PROVINCIAL JAVA – THE SUGAR INDUSTRY IN PEKALONGAN-TEGAL, 1800-1942 / G.R. Knight / isbn 90-5383-260-2 76 p.
14. ASIAN CAPITALISTS IN THE EUROPEAN MIRROR / Mario Rutten / isbn 90-5383-270-X 72 p.
15. A PEOPLE OF MIGRANTS – ETHNICITY, STATE AND RELIGION IN KARACHI / Oskar Verkaaik / isbn 90-5383-339-0 89 p.
16. COMMUNITIES AND ELECTORATES – A COMPARATIVE DISCUSSION OF COMMUNALISM IN COLONIAL INDIA / Dick Kooiman / isbn 90-5383-394-3 88 p.
17. SOCIAL SCIENCE IN SOUTHEAST ASIA – FROM PARTICULARISM TO UNIVERSALISM / Nico Schulte Nordholt and Leontine Visser (eds.) / isbn 90-5383-427-3 165 p.
18. MARTYRDOM AND POLITICAL RESISTANCE – ESSAYS FROM ASIA AND EUROPE / Joyce Pettigrew (ed.) / isbn 90-5383-501-6 146 p.
19. UNSETTLED FRONTIERS AND TRANSNATIONAL LINKAGES – NEW TASKS FOR THE HISTORIAN OF MODERN ASIA / Leo Douw (ed.) / isbn 90-5383-539-6 38 p.
20. THE SULU ZONE – THE WORLD CAPITALIST ECONOMY AND THE HISTORICAL IMAGINATION / James Francis Warren / isbn 90-5383-568-7 71 p.
21. TIME MATTERS – GLOBAL AND LOCAL TIME IN ASIAN SOCIETIES / Willem van Schendel and Henk Schulte Nordholt (eds.) / isbn 90-5383-745-0 143 p.